Frederick Griffin

The World under Glass

Frederick Griffin

The World under Glass

ISBN/EAN: 9783743310773

Manufactured in Europe, USA, Canada, Australia, Japa

Cover: Foto ©Thomas Meinert / pixelio.de

Manufactured and distributed by brebook publishing software (www.brebook.com)

Frederick Griffin

The World under Glass

BY

FREDERICK GRIFFIN,

AUTHOR OF

"The Destiny of Man," "The Storm King," and other Poems.

LONDON:

TRÜBNER & Co., LUDGATE HILL.

1879.

THE WORLD UNDER GLASS.

Crowning the brow of Sydenham Hill,
    A web-like fabric stands;
An evidence of modern skill,
    'Tis framed in iron bands;
And England's Crystal Palace
    Is the renowned of many lands.
'Twere hard at first to realise
    That from the earth there grew
What seems a fairy paradise
    Rising to realms of blue;
Whose site all others far outvies
    In its majestic view.

As nature claims the foremost place
    In all we here behold,
The landscape's features may we trace
    In outline free and bold;
And twofold skill I thus embrace,
Of Painter and of Poet's grace,
    Framed in a magic mould.

In the filmy distance far away
    Are seen the hills of Kent,
Where light and shade so often play
At sunset, near the close of day;
When here and there the shadows grey
    By roseate hues are rent.

Alike o'er hill and villaged plain
    These fitful gleams appear,
Till each in bold relief again
    Has been to thee brought near,
As though had donned fair nature's dame,
    At eve, her richest gear.

Reader! Attention, then, I crave,
    While I impress thine ear,
And on thy mind's eye would engrave
    A vision of beauty here,
Which though it be like a passing wave
Glancing o'er treasures in some dark cave
Whose waters reflect, as they gently lave,
    Its mirrored glories clear.

And now as thy guide,
In thought, by thy side,
    I start from the Anerley gate,
With intention to scan
Those relics, which man
    Has preserved of the earliest date.

But it seems passing strange,
Howe'er the world change,
    That these creatures embodied in stone
Have left so little trace
Of their name and their race,
    That the matter I must let alone.

For I cannot receive
All that sages believe
    Concerning the bones that they find,
Which are sorted at guess;
So I'm free to confess
    The subject's not clear to my mind.

With mystery 'tis smothered
How said bones were covered,
    Though each were put right in its place.
Surely scarce must be food
On rocks rugged and rude,
    While the creatures are rather obese.

For a voyage in the ark
Did all these embark?
    If so—to a new world they came.
Was it not to their taste
That they left it in haste?
    Or was their existence a name?

'Tis all mere conjecture;
Then why should I lecture
    On a subject so hazy and strange?

But of other matter,
To wit, the earth's strata,
    We will talk, as it comes in our range.

Then tell me the meaning of those black lines
Whose lowest point so deep inclines,
And a section shews of the great coal mines,
    Where the grim toilers dwell.
But 'tis few that kindle the Christmas fire,
Who think of the labour and hardship dire,
When human sinews strain and tire
For their daily portion of wage and hire,
    Which they deserve so well.

And those dear faces at that fireside,
Who ever have formed its joy and pride,
May bid defiance to wind and tide,
    When across the sea they come.
For impelled by steam the ship doth ride,
And has not the coal that steam supplied
    Which brings them swiftly home?

And for those not severed by ocean band,
Whether they journey by water or land,
In need of the fuel alike they stand,
For the iron racer with hasty stride
Devours no other food beside,
    As it madly rushes on.

Oh! wonders there are 'neath the earth untold,
    Which for ages have lain concealed;

Is it thirst for knowledge, or thirst for gold
    That has caused them to be revealed?
Or whether it be for the making of books,
Into which not a tenth of mankind ever looks;
Or whether it be with design to give,
Exercise to the tongue by which lecturers live.
That "knowledge is power" the wise folks say;
Most true it is, and I've mentioned the way
They turn it to coin, and make it pay.
But whatever the purpose of those who strive
Into earth's mysteries deep to dive,
I hope that they at the truth will arrive.

But man, how little thy vaunted strength,
    Or knowledge of unseen things!
Canst thou measure the vein of the rock's great length
    To thy mattock's blow as it rings?
Or sound the depth of the crater's base
    Whence volcanic lava springs?
And ye, who have watched the fearsome chase,
When the torrent pursues its deadly race,
    And around destruction flings;
Stupendous power full well ye know
Stirreth the demon of fire below,
    The power that rules all things.

    Now ye who peruse these varying lines,
    Be patient. I would that each verse combines
    Not alone the measure to suit the rhymes
    But a chain of thought which each branch defines.

So from gay to grave I lead the strain,
And, as we stroll onward, to gay again.

By many an undulating sweep,
Up steep incline, down hillock deep,
    Whichever way we wend,
The banks of hardy evergreen,
Half shading oft the distant scene,
    An added beauty lend.
And in the happy summer time,
The oak, the beech, and shady lime,
    Protect from sunshine's beam.
And like the frame of a mirror rare
They fringe the silver lake which there
Bears on its bosom the young and fair.
Would that as smoothly and free from care
    They might glide o'er life's troubled stream.
But hark! The peals of laughter sound.
What have we here? A vast play-ground.
How happy are some in the merry-go-round!
While others are swinging with joyous bound
    High in the fresh pure air.

'Tis a fact well known how man derives
That strength from the air, by which life revives
    And lightens that life of care.
But the games which develop the muscular power,
As well as beguile the passing hour;
These are the Englishman's manly boast
As he takes his stand by the wicket post,

With well-trained hand and practised eye,
Prepared his skill and strength to try.

But as we've described that the landscape teems
With varied shadows and sunny beams,
So the shades in descriptive outline may
By contrast enhance her beauties gay.
And thus will we clothe in poetic lay
    A lesson on duties stern ;
A lesson which to all applies
Who claim their birth 'neath English skies,
    And all alike must learn.
And to defend her then you must,
To whom her honour is in trust ;
Prompt to answer the bugle-call,
Each in his place in the ranks to fall,
Together compact as a massive wall,
Which, tested, its strength will prove.
Oh ! well may thy country depend
    That her honour is safe in thy keeping,
Inch by inch of the ground to defend,
    The laurels of glory while reaping.
To prove that British courage means,
Not the heat and flash that with instinct gleams,
    For a moment with zeal to burn ;
But a steady reliance on hand and will,
Where union is strength with soldierly drill.
His duty unflinching shall each fulfil,
For without discipline daring is nil,

When as if by one impulse stirred,
Where the word of command is heard,
As one man the columns should move.

A king once ruled in England,
    Of lion-hearted name,
And to his red-cross banner
    Her sons by thousands came.
They followed him to the Holy War;
    Faith's emblem was the sign
Of one who fought right worthily
    Of his father's royal line.

A queen now rules in England,
    All honour to her name!
While the lion-hearted title
    Her royal princes claim;
Who've nobly represented her
    Where'er her flag floats free,
Mong England's loyal subjects
    In lands beyond the sea.

Be then each man in England
    Prepared to guard her fame;
For she a soldier's duty
    From all her sons can claim.
On her lion-hearted thousands
    Victoria depends,
Whose banner still the path proclaims
    That God her right defends.

THE WORLD UNDER GLASS.

Scarce stay we a passing glance to bestow
On old history's weapons, the arrow and bow.
Not alone caused they terror to deer and to roe,
But destruction hurled on thy country's foe.
'Twas like piercing hail in a cloud of snow,
As their feathery missiles the archers throw,
Which oft the battle turn.

Across to the sunny side now let us go—
From whence the zephyrs a fragrance blow
From roses with graceful stem that twine
Round the walls, and a fairy temple line,
Which the birds make vocal in wooing note,
As their rhymeless carols in azure float.
No concert room e'er on this earth can be found
Of voices more thrilling to echo the sound;
While gorgeous ceiling and gilded dome,
But imprison the songsters, who freely would roam,
For in the blue heavens they make their home,
And saving the sky, they roof have none,
But away they speed when the music is done.

Oh! queen of all beauty, so lovely and fair,
Here no other blossom thy glory shall share
But roses of deepest crimson shade,
And those that resemble the blushing maid.

O'er the length and the breadth of the world far and wide
The Empire Celestial sends leaves curled and dried.

But here we have leaves of aroma the same,
Combined with a tinge of the sunset that came.
All these are here seen in their beauty and pride,
With some scarce removed from the hedge-row's side,
The briar, tangled and wild, nature's sweet child,
On whom the warm sunshine as brightly has smiled
As on those who were nurtured in temperature mild.

And some on bed of moss repose
Which shields from each rough blast that blows;
While others colourless and fair,
Might fitly deck the sunny hair,
Or grace the trembling hand
Of one who stakes her all of life
To claim the happy name of wife
When linked by holy band;
With roses then her path ye strew.
    Emblem that such life's path may be.
Oh! pray that thorns may there be few
And love unfading, ever true,
    Strengthen, though years may flee.

And now 'tis high holiday, happy and bright,
While I picture a scene of joy and delight.
Surely old Father Neptune his frolics doth play
As he tosses aloft the white feathery spray,
In mirrored flakes a silvery sheet,
Or broken like the winter's sleet,
Into fantastic, graceful shapes,
As each forth-rushing unfettered escapes,

Which leaping high so lightly bound,
While others in the chase are found,
In eddying gambols near the ground,
No longer restrained by iron band
But spurning the long obeyed command.

Like gladsome youth released from school
Where, curbed by so-called iron rule,
His youthful nature's sport and glee
Was there pent up, but now bursts free
With gesture and shout right merrily.
It seems that the volume of water poured
 So swift through the heated air,
Should a feeling of some relief afford
 To the holiday-makers there,
When across those terraces long and broad
 The rays of sunshine glare.

The garden of Italy this they call,
But I think that the fact is patent to all
 That Italy's sky of ethereal blue
Needs the canopied shade,
By soft breezes swayed,
 From the trees which nature grew.
And if Italy boast such a gay parterre
Combining the glory of statuary rare
 Beneath a Southern sky,
Without shelter or shade
Like that here displayed,

Would any then dare
To be sauntering there
Till the zenith of sunshine fade?
Here the critic cries "Halt!"
I've discovered a fault,
For where is the last vowel's rhyme?"
Oh! if you mean sky,
That I may rectify
When 'tis used a second time.
To climb those weary steps will tire;
Let us then rest awhile and inquire
   Whom represent they? those figures of stone,
Like sentries placed, at distances measured
As though the care of the Arts there treasured
   Was trusted to them alone,
As each apart on an eminence stands,
   Attracting the idler's gaze,
And skilful the brain as the sculptor's hands
   That could such trophies raise.

To commerce old England owes much of her power,
   Whereby she is Queen of the Sea,
And the cities that brought her so regal a dower
   Should each of them first mentioned be.

Metropolis of the North, we Manchester will name,
London's second in command which shall a notice claim;
Where fruits of thrifty industry are seen on every hand
Which find their way to every home and dwelling in the land.

But few trace to the Inventor's power
That which they're using hour by hour,
And still less can they comprehend
The thought producing such great end.

Their works the best memorial are
    Of living genius past;
Yet memory's tribute they display,
In marble, stone, or granite grey,
    As by the sculptor cast.

From countries and cities, all these take a name,
But who gave those countries and cities their fame,
So that each forms a radius of good to mankind
And contributes to art and to pleasure combined?
'Twas the men who adorned them by greatness of mind.

'Tis right to acknowledge then gratitude's debt
By means the most lasting, so none may forget.
A long list of creditors truly have ye
From whom England gained wealth both by land and by sea,
And the means to defend those riches shall be,
Black Birmingham, ever supplied by thee.

    'Twas in the days of the old Crusade
    Men trusted the good Damascus blade,
    But Sheffield now supplies the steel,
    Of knighthood oft the badge and seal.

    And England's fair sister, the Isle of the Sea
    Contributes her share of use to thee,

Which the housewife stores so thriftily;
For linen, fair as the wintry snows,
Which takes its name from the damask rose,
The industry of Belfast shews.

Then England's colonies each by name
Shall now a triple mention claim.
Australia with stores of wealth untold,
And country that baffles the explorer bold.
And India, the gorgeous, whose wealth and extent
Has material raw to Britain lent.
Yes, lent, I say; for the conquered hate
The conqueror, who ne'er can subjugate
Their will, and the rites of creed and caste,
Though ye may regard their treachery past;
But vengeance has surely an unpaid debt
Where exists there a mosque or a minaret.

To follow the course of the rising sun,
As in the east was our task begun,
To the west we must journey ere it be done,
To the land of snows where the merry sleigh bells
    Vibrating through the air,
The spirit of freedom their music tells
As away down the slopes, and up from the dells,
    With an impetus on they dare.

Oh! a hardy race are the Canada men
    Resembling their ice-bound shore;
Their dwellings supplied from the pine-tree glen,
    Their music the rapid's roar.

And now we have mentioned the threefold source
    Of England's foreign sway,
'Tis meet that a tribute to each we endorse,
    Which here these statues display.

Is not beauty thine essence, O land of France?
E'en since the days of the tilt and lance,
    And the Field of the Cloth of Gold,
Thy fabrics may justly their claims advance
    The form of our dames to enfold.

Thy turbulent neighbour, the kingdom of Spain,
    The next in succession appears.
And here we've a stronghold of England again
    Which a stern rugged face e'er uprears.
It stands to keep guard o'er the sea's highway
    Above that ancient town,
While those who pass 'neath the rocks of grey
The answering signal there display
    To the standard of England's crown.

Oh! country of golden sunshine,
    Italy, Mother of Art;
Nor could we any branch define
    In which thou bear'st not a part.
The tones of thy language gracefully tell
    Of music's enchanting power,
While painting and sculpture the catalogue swell
To refine, and the gloom of the world to dispel,
    Where clouds too often lower.

And next in the list of Southern climes
Is one who can boast, from the earliest times,
That she bears the palm where genius shines.
'Tis of classic Greece—whose praise I sing,
While now the flight of time doth bring
To modern Greece a youthful king,
With whom we trust that all good may abide,
As England by marriage to him is allied.

With Oriental pomp and state
The Sultan's dominions challenge debate;
And the domes of those ancient cities rise
In myriads of varied height and size,
O'ershadowing the sable sea that lies
Beyond the bounds of the narrow strait,
Defending like a fortress-gate
The realms of that turbaned potentate.

    Then pause a moment while we trace,
    In due rotation in this place,
    What ancient Egypt can unfold
    By her vast pyramids of old,
    And which, according to the sages,
    Erected were in by-gone ages—
    Say, some four thousand years ago,
    As symbols with design to shew
    A forethought, calculation proving,
    In the power their builder moving;
    Whereby the measurement, 'tis clear

THE WORLD UNDER GLASS.

Is like to this world's solar year;
Though 'twas reserved for later time
The secret meaning to define,
And divers theories to propound
From mystic signs which here are found,
The wise and learnèd to confound.

As we with nature's work began,
And led you on to that which man
Has deftly wrought 'neath Heaven's wide span
    To grace the fair earth's face,
And 'neath the walls of that mansion clear
E'en now we stay to linger here,.
Scanning the beauties far and near
    That memory may retrace.

But now into the world of glass,
With the admiring crowds we pass;
A world indeed, which here can boast
Of all that world should honour most,
Refinement, science, cultured art;
All these have their allotted part.

The earth's four quarters hither meet
    Their treasures to compare,
And form a nucleus most complete,
    Ye seek in vain elsewhere.

Of priceless relics rich the store
Which never copied were before,

Whose due proportions fitly placed
With all by Time's rough hand defaced;
And sculptured greatness lives again
Though Corinth's towers be rent in twain,
While th' Adriatic's seven-throned Queen,
Shews what her grandeur once had been,
And chronicles boast an unbroken record
Of all that has perished by fire and by sword,
And of treasures long buried, to us here restored.

But stay—let us on the threshold pause
    Of an open door, which invites
To enter the dwelling—and first read the clause
Of one who guards with iron jaws
    The Pompeian nobleman's rights.
Fit guard for a home deserted
    In effigy he appears;
By him now alone asserted
    Are the rights of former years;
While strangers the marble entry tread
    As vacant is their stare,
As the rooms now are, in which 'tis said
Dwelt those, long numbered with the dead,
    When they claimed of the earth their share.

To scenes of sacred history
    In order next we turn,
Though few can fathom the mystery,
    Or themselves with the study concern,

To unravel the hidden meaning
    In hieroglyphics veiled,
Though the Bible light in its beaming
    Has already the darkness assailed,
On the symbols of Nineveh's glory
    Whose models from thence were exhumed,
Sole proof of the direful story
    That an earthquake the city consumed—
And thus with the light of ages
    We value th' explorer's toil,
Which lends to the ancient pages
A reality which engages
    The mind in reflection's coil.

Now pass we into an open space,
Where many gorgeous colours grace,
And golden lines the figures trace,
    In architectural form.
Can the sable Moor whose flashing eye
Seems to reflect a thunder sky,
    Foreboding angry storm,
Can he artistic thought express?
Then marvel not if we digress,
Just admiration to confess,
In terms that scarcely can be less
Than as those colours warm.

For aided by fancy's mystical powers,
With the senses regaled by sweet scented flowers,

As the fountain murmurs in silver showers,
'Twould seem that a day-dream again delights
    Its enchanted spell to weave.
And thought flies back to Arabian nights,
When that hall was illumined by thousand lights
    On a brilliant *fête* at eve.

To aid the illusion a tropical clime
    By means artificial is made,
So that here in the gloom of our long winter time
    There is foliage that never will fade,
On whose beauties we linger in triplicate rhyme,
    While we rest 'neath the trees' leafy shade.

When ye as children learnt at schools
    The sound without the meaning,
Then were ye not likened to parrots or fools?
    Though 'twas but of joy ye were dreaming,
While happy and bright as a bird on the wing
Thought fled away like a fairy thing?

But here, in dazzling plumage drest,
The parrots greet the passing guest,
Who oft with kind caress and smile
The feathered captive's life beguile;
For never again in the clear blue sky
Those lovely pinions may soar on high.
Could nature, who gave them the power of speech,
Bring the range of thought within their reach,
Oh! then they could tell of a pathway paved

With rays of light, as in sunshine bathed,
Which the gossamer clouds but scarcely veiled,
As away through the air they gracefully sailed.

But that bright life is a dream gone by ;
Now a crystal canopy forms their sky,
And to break their chain 'tis in vain to try,
So compassion they claim from the passers by.

But who are these fluttering overhead,
    Who timidly perch, and then away?
Is it of thee that they are in dread,
    Or fear they yon fountain's spray?
From tropical climes they are hither brought ;
    And surely their plumage gay,
Like the rainbow reflected, a shade has caught
    From the dazzling sunshine's ray.
Here shelter the sparrows from Java's isle,
    Who would die if let go free;
While their English namesakes for many a mile
With wing untiring their life beguile
    In the blessing of liberty.

The native hedge-sparrow, sturdy and strong,
Is hardy as those he lives among.
His numerous race thrives in every place
That forms a part of the earth's broad face,
Like the men who a Saxon ancestry trace.

But now 'tis time that we descend
    From the flight of our thoughts in the air,

And through a door at the eastern end
    Let us follow the long broad stair
Which leads to the world beneath the sea,
Where inquiring thought may wander free
    Among the dwellers there.

Shall we now the corridor long describe,
    Or turn to the frames of glass,
Behind which the pictures are breathing things
    Regarding us as we pass?
In silence they may leap and dance
Or tamely view with looks askance
Those who with wondering heads advance,
    And whom science hither brings.

Of varied race are the finny tribe
    In their coats of silver lining,
And when with headlong plunge they dive,
The ripples from off their scaly back
Like a stream of pearls now mark their track,
    When the noontide sun is shining.
And as each tank is filled to the brim
And fresh air from without is supplied within,
So day after day they do nothing but swim.

All save the lobsters, whose coat of mail,
Seems to weigh them down like a top-heavy sail,
And they, like the divers under the sea,
    Enjoy a respiration free;

So majestic in promenade they stalk,
And all the day long they do nothing but walk.

In piscatorial order placed
Are here arranged with skill and taste,
   The swimmers large and small.
But one from the list might be erased,
   For he swimmeth not at all.
'Tis he who derives his name
   From graceful locomotion;
And of none can we say the same
   Throughout the boundless ocean.
For it matters not to the hardy skate
Whether the season be early or late,
Or whether it be in frost or in thaw.
Such has ever been nature's law;
And so it will always be their fate
All the day long to do nothing but skate.

But now come hither, I'll let you see
How two kingdoms allied can be,
Without a monarch o'er either to reign.
Together they live, nor dare complain
Where so slight a boundary divides them twain.

Next, then, there seems a point of debate.
Is it breath from without can agitate
The flower whose cup of tender down
So gently trembles from base to crown?

Examine and see if there be any chink,
And none you'll discover, I surely think,
Where the zephyr's faintest sigh can shew
The life of the plants among fishes that grow.

Are there lungs within, the air to inflate
Or can it be said to vegetate?
Though with animal senses all entire
To be found among weeds of the marsh and mire,
Companions strange for one whose name
As a garden ornament may claim,
To be numbered with flowers of purple and red,
Nurtured with care in a cultured bed,
And the flowering anemone blooms in pride
While its briny namesake is tossed by the tide.
But the kingdom of him who comes from the sea
Is higher, proud flower, than belongs to thee,
For the animal world with him begins.
Then have we dumb creatures propelled by fins
But deaf they are not, for surely they
Can hear the tiny rivulet play
    As it tosses them o'er and o'er;
And when the angry storm draws near
Why close to the shore their course they steer
    Warned by the billow's roar.

Now remark that the lowest order of things
That possess a voice are those with wings,
By whom alone 'tis in melody used,
But never in discord the gift is abused.

And now from our subject a moment we'll stray
To gather from birds who are winging their way,
A moral to lighten the cares of to-day ;
And as we have seen that for harmony sweet
    The gift of a voice was intended,
Oh ! 'tis surely but right when together ye meet
    That with kindness thine accents be blended.
Who knows not the sound of a gentle tone
That rules by the power of persuasion alone ?

  Ask the lover and he will tell ;
  Who softly pleadeth, pleadeth well.
  Ask of the youth, whose voice now rings
    Through the vaulted roof o'erhead,
  To tell of the joy such laughter brings
    And like the roses red,
The health flush on his boyish cheek,
With the sparkle and fire of his eye, bespeak
That though of industry much may be said,
Yet by relaxation is intellect fed ;
And when he to classical books returns,
Why see how quickly the task he learns ;
And so aptly the problem of distance discerns
That commendation just he earns
For making a circle and square agree,
That puzzle to young humanity.

But ere from the subject we retire,
Be ye admonished to acquire

Some knowledge of products, which daily bestow
The blessings from grain up-springing that grow,
For the staff that human life sustains
Is garnered within these golden grains,
While the oats and the barley, the beans and the rye
Their quota of animal life supply.
And thus in retrospect we're brought,—
To the subject of our previous thought,
The alliance, I mean, of the kingdoms twain,
On which we have once to remark again
That though the status of one be higher
Yet its existence doth require
From the other, supplies, as fuel to fire,
Without which vitality there must expire;
While that kingdom which holds the lower place
On no other depends for continued race,
For 'tis nourished alone by the power unseen
And needs no aid to come between.
'Tis true no creature on earth may know
How the tender flower and the sapling grow,
But one such mystical food may share,
Discernèd not yet everywhere.
That one is the spiritual being of soul
Expanding under Divine control
And gaining wisdom as ages roll.

Would you instance the scope of human mind
With learning and poetry both combined?
Then turn to him whose dwelling here

Recalls a name to England dear,
The bard of the Avonside—William Shakespeare.
    His genius like that river,
    In even current flowed ;
    And proverbs living ever
    Had birth in this quaint abode.
How brilliant the fire of his wit, I ween,
In the comedy's mirth exciting scene,
As the ripples that dance upon Avon's stream,
When lit by the rosy sunset's beam,
Sparkling awhile—then dying away,
Like the joyous burst of that laughter gay.

    Then after the sun has vanished,
        And the long dark shadows fall,
    For awhile is that brightness banished
        Which thy spirit held in thrall ;
    And a more impressive feeling
        Gives place—while all around
    To the soft illusion yielding
        Are bathed in a gloom profound.
    There's a charm in the evening stillness
        When nature sinks to sleep,
    Though her voice of night be songless
        As the pathos of tragedy deep.

    With power which has the soul entranced,
    The purpose and plot by each scene advanced
        In rapt attention keep

The audience, as though spell-bound,
While not one harsh discordant sound,
    May there intruding creep.

Oh! I could with fire and with energy write
    Of dramatical genius displayed,
By him whose shrewd wisdom in proverbs now trite,
    With his memory never will fade!
Did I in biographal ode wish to shine,
Here are models by dozens the task to incline;
But I have to do with the present scene,
And can only glance at the days that have been,
With a word here and there of instruction between,
Which we from the harvest of intellect glean.

Then next we come to the transept space,
Where pleasure holds the right of place;
And 'neath *his* dwelling to whom it owes
The debt of fame which ever grows,
    The mighty stage uprears.
Though in the cosy Christmas time
It may be used for pantomime,
    Which that chill season cheers,
To harlequin and columbine
The parts to each one we assign;
    While mirth and jest go round,
And happy faces full of glee
With wonder gaze, that there should be
    Such marvels to be found.

THE WORLD UNDER GLASS.

But glad surprise with wonder share
When to the view a scene so fair
All glowing is presented, where
The fairies poised as if in air
    Their radiant charms unfold ;
While every tree and floweret there
    Is bathed in shining gold.
'Tis as if to the world of beauty and grace
In day-dreams ye're wafted to dwell for a space,
And ye would the aid of the fairies invoke,
To invite longer stay among such pleasant folk.
But alas ! there's a solemn green curtain of baize,
Which descending will hide that bright world from thy gaze.
Then begone ! to thine every-day world and its ways,
The lights are extinguished, and each one obeys.

    But invoke we inspiration,
    Now with thrilling deep sensation,
    Born alone of Heaven's creation,
        Where the muse doth dwell ;
    Music tends to consecration
    Of the heart, in adoration,
        On the organ's swell ;
    While her softer modulation,
    How it soothes to supplication,
        As by solemn spell.

    When first the voice of harmony
        Vibrated on the lyre,

It wakened in the ancient bards
    The heart's poetic fire.
And earth-born voices mingled
    With the ethereal choir,
Whose echoes hither wafted
    Swept o'er the golden wire.
'Twas meet the world's first harmony
    Should dedicated be
To Him who gave the birds a song
    Of boundless joy and glee.
Away to the clear blue heaven they rise,
    On pinion light and free;
Melody carrying through the skies
    Wherewith to gladden thee.

Was it from them that Jubal gained,
    The thought producing sound,
From instruments made of the forest trees
    And metal from 'neath the ground?
And when the very air he breathed,
    Th' inventor's triumph crowned.
'Twas Nature, yielding to his will,
    That the materials found,
And aided the colossal mind
By whom the organ was designed.

Since then, to many thousand hearts
    Is Jubal's name endeared,

For he who sacred sounds first raised,
    Should justly be revered.
Soft as the vocal breath of prayer
    From human voices poured,
Its modulations soothe the soul,
    And thrill each inmost chord.
'Till diapason's echoes sweep
   Through the vast space in thunders deep.
While in melodious cadence
    Orchestral music peals.
Away from the sorrows and cares of life
    The spirit of man it steals,
To dream of a world where love's own balm
    The wounded spirit heals.

Lo! the echo of children's voices
    Ascends through transept and nave,
And each sound, as youth rejoices,
    Rolls on, like the distant wave,
As music's loveliest anthems rise
In swelling cadence towards the skies.

Oh! surely unseen harps of gold
Echo the song of praise that is told,
And many a holy thought they bear
Far away through the distant air,
Where tones of love may penetrate
E'en past the portal of Heaven's gate.

Of those who music's festivals attend
Some to be so-called critics oft pretend;
While many only come because by custom led,
Although the love of music brought them there, 'twas said.
Others attracted are by that which charms the sense;
But few have gained a higher thought that comes they know
    not whence,
Unseen as that world of which it tells,
Resembling some far-distant chime of bells,
Whose melody, as it may rise and fall,
Rests here and there, but is not heard by all.
How little know ye, then, what magnet 'twas that drew
Th'enormous crowds of whom 'tis said but few
Were prompted by love's highest impulse true.

Methinks 'twere surely right that in the realms of space
Music of sacred type should hold the foremost place;
And from the early records its history thus we trace;
But now to thee in verse I would convey
Impression clear of music, grave and gay;
Where every instrument is turned to suit the measure.
It fills the senses with delight and pleasure;
Softly at first the swelling chords ascend,
Until the instruments with voices blend;
How glorious then the sounds which they aloft can send!

    Oh! muse of Heaven! In thee alone to share
    With angels in the music of their world so fair,
    Is privilege to be esteemed far higher
    'Than aught on earth to which ye can aspire;

For although all unheard is their melody's sound,
Yet influence harmonious here surely is found,
As the musical echoes vibrate around.

It is music in the highest sense of which we here have spoken,
And of her universal power we next produce the token;
For 'tis she who rules the spirit
And who seldom fails to win it,
Captive leading inclination
By her charm of fascination;
While they the nation's songs who render
Best proclaim how to defend her;
And thus they serve their country's cause,
As well as those who make her laws;
For they who can originate
The noble songs which animate
To every impulse brave and great,
They are the men who legislate.

Would I mention all that music combines,
How its soul-ennobling power refines
    Where'er its echoes fall,
A volume at least to melodious tone
I should need to devote to description alone;
    And therefore I would but recall
How the soldier of fortune it ofttimes cheers
While the veteran's step so light appears,
As though he'd regained the strength of years,

When the bugle's summoning voice he hears
    Or the life-stirring sound of the drum ;
And where the zeal of the young recruit,
All glowing and fresh as his brilliant suit,
If the many-tongued martial band were mute,
    Which marks their tramp as they come.
And when o'er the deep his course to steer,
While leaving home, kindred, and country dear,
'Tis music bold salt-water Jack can cheer,
As triumphant she tells how Britannia rides
On the waves she rules—while her strength abides
Not alone in impregnable iron-sides,
But the iron will of her sons besides,
Whose coolness in danger the good ship guides.

    O Music, 'tis thine insidious part,
        The human mind to sway,
    For thou canst poise the Love-god's dart,
        'Neath the guise of a ballad gay.
    While in the still and silent night
        Are breathed in serenade
    Those vows that with the dawn of light
        Be sure will never fade.
    Or it may be as down the stream ye glide
        At the close of a summer's day;
    That music soft as the rippling tide,
        Love's secret will betray.

Now having here three points combined
Where music's power can rule the mind,

Religion, patriot zeal, and love,
It but remains for us to prove
How music's power the world can move;
And how, from infancy to age,
'Tis that which cheers life's every stage.
It charms young fancy, and the mind doth lead
To that repose the aged ofttimes need;
Of savage tribes the sole refining power,
And neath whose charm e'en poisonous reptiles cower.
What marvel, then, if nature's nobler creatures
(Who often might be made man's moral teachers)
Should further of this power an evidence supply!
Go, ask the soldier, when the trumpet's cry
Summons to duty—let him tell thee why
His mettled steed that proud crest tosses high;
Assuring his rider, with answering neigh,
That both ready and willing is he to obey;
Or mark how he lists to the measured beat,
As with action high he lifts his feet;
Let the march be quick, let the march be slow,
To step to the time full well does he know,
And nature's instinct for music shew.

And when the shrill blast of the huntsman's horn,
O'er mead and hollow by echoes borne,
Quick to obey by leap and bound
Breaks from the covert the gallant hound;
    Then away in full cry,
    All restraint they defy,

And from each eager throat,
Comes the answering note,
While the horn's clear sounds through the air that float
Their power o'er the canine brain denote,
Whose musical voices again inspire
Horseman and horse with intrepid fire.
Like sheath of arrows abroad dispersed
Has the first flight over the landscape burst.
Nor regard they the dangers which over they fly
While forward! hark forward! the rallying cry.

And now the effect from its cause to trace,
Return we from the exciting chase,
And remember ye then, ere the pack off threw,
That the musical blast which the huntsman blew
Was the source whence this fiery ardour grew.

And such the powers all other powers excelling,
Whose subtle influence savage natures quelling,
Proves that stern passions thus may be assailed
When other means to tame them all have failed;
Where menaced threat and voice cannot command,
'Tis there that music lifts her magic wand.
As by a charmèd wave the air they breathe she fills,
Till every nerve and pulse of their wild being thrills.
Again, the power of sound applies to undeveloped mind,
When ye peruse the legends strange taught to the infant kind
Whose fabled language erst conveyed in rhyme
Awakes in childhood's ear its mirth exciting chime,

And though in fiction clothed the fables may appear,
Yet thus disguised a fact may be of worthy mention here.

So without further prelude now the story I begin
Of puss, and that small instrument we term the violin;
The only instrument I know of two-fold appellation,
And which, familiarly expressed in common conversation,
By homely phraseology is likewise called the fiddle,
Though whence the derivation springs to me remains a riddle.
And next, the substance of this tale a doubt may well provoke,
But which I challenge ye to test ere treated as a joke,
For all know well who've legends read
That to the feline quadruped,
The poor domestic harmless cat,
High pranks were oft imputed,
And comic though the tale may be, it ne'er has been refuted.
Thus says tradition, sorely scared,
The cow, who in the pastime shared,
Leapt o'er the moon, but no one cared;
And whether from fright or playful glee
May still be a mystery to you and me;
But wildly she ran, with bound and spring
On hearing the sound of the cat-gut string;
From this one inference only I draw,
'Tis that nature's universal law
Points to music alone as the witching art
In which every intelligent being has part.
'Tis true that some animal painters we style,
But 'tis men—not the brutes—that we mean all the while.

By the latter such talent is counted as naught,
But their love for sweet sound needs not to be taught.

On music then I have laid some stress
At the risk of your thinking that I digress;
Because it is that which enlivens the whole
Of the other subjects we here enroll;
And this bright crystal world so fair
Devoid of artistic music rare,
Amid beauties of nature by none surpassed,
Would be but a sombre museum vast,
Which, though for the student containing rich treasures,
To the holiday-maker affording few pleasures.
But now look around the concert-room gay;
For within, as without, can nature display
What painter or sculptor can never pourtray—
The intelligent brightness of youthful faces,
The living resemblance of Muses and Graces,
At every festival the honoured guest
'Tis music ever gives to joy a zest,
Then she, as Queen of Muses, surely stands confessed.

But now it is time that we onward should stroll,
Where the fine arts combine to embellish the whole
Of the courts which appear in constant succession,
While of some information the mind gains possession.

For the ornamental, the chaste, and refined
Look then to France; for 'tis there are designed

Inventions which pander to luxury's taste,
And some here restored, which past centuries graced;
For instance, the style of Louis Quatorze!
How divers the specimens sent to these shores.

Did I say that for holiday-makers alone
Was this high favoured spot? Why then I must own
An error in judgment for which I atone
By leading you now to where literature's worth
Sheds its light o'er the world, through morocco and cloth;
From brains highly cultured, the fruit garnered there,
Long produce of years, of study and care.
Here flowery thoughts are "immortelles" made,
Which for ages have flourished, nor yet will fade,
While their beauty remains still undecayed
Though the hand that grafted them death has stayed.
Some by the force of bold rhetoric's storm
Which its authors intended the world should reform,
Have gained undying fame, attached to their name,
And smile at the critics who praise, or who blame.

And others there are whose gifted mind
Gave expression to thought which, with verse combined,
Though it may not reform, has the world refined.
Some of these have been creditors long to mankind.
I allude to the poets; to whom belong
Dramatic enchantment and power of song;
Entertainers are they of the crowded throng,
And though seen not, may yet be those crowds among.

Now some, 'tis said, the midnight oil consume,
Which expression interpreted means, I presume,
That they more easy mental food digest
When all the outer world is lulled to rest,
Companioned then in silent array
By the authors whose knowledge their works convey.
See, the latter are with thee in long, straight ranks,
And the spirits which breathed them should claim thy thanks.
Is not genius immortal then, I repeat?
For 'tis in the soul that it hath its seat.
Indestructible surely that throne must be
To last throughout eternity.

  In thoughts like these away we soar,
    Following swift on fancy's flight;
  And to earth returned once more
    Enter we a scene all bright;
  And here is a question for you to decide,
  For I'm of opinion that being allied
    To the great world ye live in by name,
  Is an honour to which of right ye aspire;
  I speak now of that which in sparkle and fire
  Resembles the diamond, proud beauty's attire,
    For crystal and glass are the same.
  Then think of the dazzling graces untold,
  Which the mirror reflects a hundred fold;
  While those who frequently look within,
  By that means hoping something to win,
  Which melts in the grasp of its votaries proud

Like the evening sun in a misty shroud;
Admiration, I mean, which makes them believe
That it can never, oh! never deceive.
Judge ye then, how the useful can be misapplied,
For glass is a product whose use is world-wide,
And without it no banquet can e'er be complete,
No toilet of beauty becoming and neat.

While beside it are gems of painting rare,
On a surface smooth as the snowdrift fair;
And colours that vie with the clouds aloft,
Are blended with those of earth's carpet soft;
Representing, it may be, the landscape's face,
Or the velvet flowers which that landscape grace;
While porcelain, like crystal, the feast will adorn,
Though it cannot reflect fair beauty's form;
Yet both taste the sweets of her ruby lips,
And 'tis from the porcelain she oftener sips;
While the crystal may vainly to pleasure excite,
Its allurements the stronger sex likewise invite,
But beware! I pray, as that glass goes round,
Wherein man's gift of intellect ofttimes is drowned,
That you be not one of those victims found.

See then how this subject can aptly teach
To man and to woman a moral for each.
The last should be first for courtesy's sake,
As I pray thee a word of advice to take.
'Tis flattery feeds thy self-conceit,
Which knows not when with food replete,

And whether provoking a censure or smile,
It passes unheeding all the while.

Let those who their mirror consult have a care
That expression contented they always find there,
To charm and to please; then none need despair,
Although others appear more dazzlingly fair.
Then lay well to heart the advice here conveyed,
For time will thy zenith of loveliness fade.

From all that the arts, or that taste can produce,
O'er a still wider subject the mind we unloose.
As we journey far over the ocean's wide track,
In retrospect now would I carry thee back,
To the time when the country I write of was trod
By those who of birthright alone claimed the sod:
Aboriginal owners, as roving and free,
As the air that they breathed or the uncontroll'd sea,
Whose countless creatures leap and bound
To the music of ocean's unceasing sound;
While the gleeful birds that through ether float
Their life in the air to joy devote.
But none of these more happy can be
Than the natives beneath the old gum tree;
Whose friendly bark their Miamis form
The dwelling that shelters from wind and storm.

Soft the language nature taught them,
    She their life needs all provided;

Clothing, shelter, food she brought them,
   And the use by instinct guided.
But ne'er to progress they aspire ;
As the son so was the sire ;
And, when each man's course is run,
As the sire will be the son.
But the pale-visaged race from the far away west
Lays claim to the land that once natives possessed.
It was no mean possession, so easy to yield,
Rich in broad pasture land and alluvial field,
Nor e'en had Dame Nature conveyed them a hint
That deep in the earth there existed a mint ;
And all her vast treasures of fortune revealed,
Could they have defended with spear and with shield.
In the science of Mars all untutored are they,
Although when excited their tribes display
An aspect ferocious, or cunning, or dread,
As by each hostile passion their courage is fed.
For instance I picture their war-dance wild,
Or "Corroboree" by the natives so styled ;
By their voices accompanied, guttural and gruff,
With music from skins untanned and rough
As the warriors weird, whose tramp is set
And timed by the uncouth castanet.
These rites have a meaning ye may not know,
When vindictive and fierce their features grow,
With their weapons waving to and fro,
It would seem as if some desperate foe
Were felled to the earth unseen below,

And savage delight deals the deadly blow.
Till with strength exhausted they strife forego.

In the lurid light of the fire sticks red
The " Corroboree " lasts till time has fled,
And then long after the set of sun
A softer sequel may be begun—
As young birds flutter beneath the tree
From the parent nest when about to flee,
And timorous crouch, nor dare to fly
Till they confidence gain and the future try.
See now at the foot of yon gum tree old
Draped in their furs with graceful fold,
Loobras of tender years behold !
Awaiting the summons of love are they
Soon to be borne as brides away.
Their hearts are throbbing 'twixt joy and fear
As the painted warriors approach them near.

Are they willing to part from childhood's kin
Ere the days of womanhood begin ?
Yes, they watch the dance with look half shy
Yet merriment beams in their bright, dark eye ;
Grouped thus in grotesque attitude
Where none but the dancers may intrude.

Let not the prying pale face dare
In those mystic rites to seek a share,
But heed their menaced threat " Forbear!"
Who for man's life but lightly care.

The wooing that's short—it has ever been said—
Is happier than that which delays to wed,
But love's declaration is here most concise
Where a smile and a seizure appear to suffice.

'Tis sensational truly, you justly reply,
And a summary measure, I don't deny,
Although human nature, imperfect always,
Becometh not better by Cupid's delays.

 Further and wider year by year,
  Australia's power extends;
 Though not by boomerang nor spear
  Her freedom she defends.
 In conscious manly dignity
  Her natives tread the soil,
 Which from them never can exact
  The tax of servile toil.
 Of ambition they dream not
  Whose wants are so few
 Nor inventive power
  With discoveries new
 Ever in their wild nature grew.

But as the sable night at dawn exists no more
So vanishes the black man's race the white man's race
 before,
And civilising light has broke on that far-distant shore,
So changed is now the earth they loved from the aspect it
 once wore,

'That earth which is man's heritage and first of the elements four;
While the air that upholds the wild bird's wing,
When he has no bough on which to cling,
Is the great vitalising force
Ever fresh from its hidden source.
All life depends on that constant supply,
For without it the flowers like the animals die;
And that which gives sweetness and bloom to the rose
Men feel in each breath from heaven that blows.
Around thee, above thee, beyond thy control,
The unseen acts on thine unseen soul.

    The two first elements, earth and air,
    Are those in which all nations share;
    Like the second, unseen, is the third ye know,
    Till its presence ye summon with one swift blow,
    Like the wizard who strikes with magic wand,
    And produces his wish by a wave of his hand.
    But the savage was never taught to acquire
    This simple process to kindle a fire.

    A grass-tree cane by him is laid,
    Horizontally fixed, and an aperture made,
    Inserted in which is the ditto upright,
    Which measures some three or four feet in height;
    And now, like steam power, in the outstretched palm,
    By rotatory motion of hand and arm,
    As swift as thought the grass cane turns,
    'Till the pith within ignited burns.

So a practical lesson the by-stander learns,
And result of patient toil discerns;
But fire unrestrained is like angry will,
Which a calmer element only can still.
May the spirit that once the blue waves pressed
Infuse love's fire in the savage breast,
And turbulent passions from thence expel,
As fire can never with water dwell.

But too long from our subject perhaps we have strayed.
Who should study the objects before us displayed,
In thought bear me company then all who will,
And behold here a scene that should make thy heart thrill
With pride for the men that to England belong,
Who have risked their own lives as avengers of wrong.
  Then 'tis to these so nobly great
  Genius and Art we dedicate,
  And thus their deeds perpetuate
   In this poetic strain.
  Brave winners of Victoria's Cross,
  The units of that armèd force
   Who Britain's power maintain.

As painting and verse for this end have combined,
 And the name of "Desanges" leads the van,
Let us honour the genius of him who designed
 To honour his brave fellow man,
Nor in haste turn away from that silent array,
For gratitude none claim more surely than they
Who boldly for England fought first in the fray.

To whom owe ye the freedom this moment enjoyed,
But to those who the foes of thy country destroyed,
And provide the insurance for wealth and broad lands?
Then forget not the premium such safety demands
But ever to those ungrudgingly give
Who have purchased thy right unmolested to live.
Thy prosperous commerce their sacrifice earned
When valour and courage the battle tide turned,
And while yours the result, be the cause well discerned.

A subject so varied now opens before us,
'Twould in music be known as a sort of a chorus;
While softened harmony of tone,
In music dwelleth not alone.
But in colouring blended as nature has taught,
And the artists who ever her guidance have sought
Are those who take rank in the foremost grade,
For their models no human hand has made.
Borne along in the chariot of fame to toil,
Whose wheels may advance through the medium of oil,
They study the world in various phases
And such contemplation the intellect raises.
Scenes of peace, or of war, picturesque or sublime,
Are by them represented, to last for all time.

'Tis needless, I think, to drag into debate
The remains of the masters of ancient date,
Whose works are all that is left of them here.
Why then if ye praise not in silence revere.

Remember, too, that those now admired,
When life's short term has with them expired,
The roll of years will alike transform,
And old masters they'll be to a world unborn,
Whose works, now modern, thy walls adorn.

Oh, scenes of regal beauty passing fair
    Described in the early chronicler's page,
The tournament gay, and the pageant rare,
    By painting transmitted from age to age
    With every scene that marketh this world's varied stage!
Thus have we here in illustrative form
    The warlike passions that mankind engage
With fascinating zeal the soul of youth to warm
That he may dare the front of battle strife and storm,
And deeds of matchless bravery by sea and land perform.
Or if to represent the ever-changing sea
    It is the artist's aim his skill to prove,
Ocean inanimate! 'tis strange that thou canst be
    Made to appear as elements that move.

And there are those who have dared to tread
The regions of fathomless ice, in dread
Of the creatures that roam o'er that cheerless field,
Where pasture is not, their food to yield.
No blade of grass relieves the eye,
And scarce in the distance they descry
The white bear, as he draweth nigh.

In a fettered girdle there lieth the ship,
By the elements seized in an icy grip,
By whose stern will were her crew immured,
Whose lives on such venture should be insured,
For the sake of those than their lives far dearer.
Say, how can I render the subject clearer?

O daughters of England, applaud them with me,
The noble, the bold-hearted sons of the sea!
Geography and history thy school-mates were together,
Bound in the scholar's memory as by a common tether,
And yolk-fellows they still are made
When summoned each to lend their aid,
To artist touch of light and shade.

As well 'twere to attempt the world to traverse round,
If ye reality would test in all that here is found;
The gorgeous sunset of the East which frames the desert's bound,
The region of eternal snows, where hushed thy footfall's sound;
And yonder Alpine monarchs in lofty grandeur crowned,
By human foot untrod, the earth-life they disown,
As they to Heaven approach, with her mantle o'er them thrown,
  While, glancing on those icy peaks,
  The sunbeams fall in rosy streaks,
  So dazzling scarce can ye behold
  The scenes which parted clouds unfold.

But yet 'tis here the artist's touch, 'tis here the poet's pen,
Uplift thee in their imag'ry above the world of men.
Aye, further, higher still, where deeper mystery shrouds,
Dare they to pierce the cold grey veil beyond the sailing clouds;
But Nature's painting ceases here, for model had they none,
Who by soul-poetry alone their heavenly task begun:
And thus a power unseen by man
    Has here been brought to bear,
And ta'en of things beyond the span
    Of earth, or sea, or air,
    Whereby they represent to thee angelic beings fair.
Oh! may not souls unconscious soar,
And, dreaming, that glad world explore,
    And of its fruits there earning
Genius produces us the store
    Though few its source discerning,
    But place the debt as credited to tutored human learning.

But when with things spiritual we have to deal
'Tis spirit alone that such can reveal;
And as like begets like 'mongst thy brethren here,
So thine essence of soul bringeth kindred souls near.
How varied the gifts that they hitherward bring
As garlands of beauty around thee to fling,
When poetry wafted on Fancy's light wing,
With music maketh thy spirit to sing.
And in this I think ye must all be agreed,
That music and painting equally need

The refinement of soul-created power,
Which, like sunshine shed on the humble flower,
Maketh its beauty and grace to expand;
And discerned are the gifts, although unseen the hand
Whose silent influence none may withstand,
For exerted it is by Divine command.

Said a sage of old that nothing new
Beneath the sunshine ever grew,
And therefore somewhat strange it seems
That this same sun should be the means
Or agent whereby ye acquire an art
Which perpetuity can impart
To the features of those ye love so well,
And whom with you only a while can dwell.
For 'tis nature herself reflected here
Indelibly fixed on the camera clear,
And by chemistry perfected year by year.
'Twas not long ago when possessing a share
Of the world of art was a privilege rare,
But accorded to those who had wealth to spare;
And denied to the humbler in means, whose mind
The influence needed of taste refined,
To allure them from tastes of a grosser kind.
But now Photography offers to these
Not only the semblance of things that please
    The eye and the mind of all;
But lo! from out the camera door
Glide forms where there was naught before,
    Like the spirits at Manfred's call—

But unlike these, in silence they,
Unheeding all ye do and say,
Once summoned, not to be dismissed,
The changeful years their forms resist,
Whose passive lips have ne'er confessed
That they by a lover in youth were pressed,
Whose form, like theirs, may be now at rest.
One moment more, to that give place
Which to biography lends its grace;
As by such light, ye read the soul
And study the feelings, which there control.
As the germ of a fruit, they will ne'er decay
But develop in actions which still convey
An example for good mankind to sway.
I write of those who can write no more;
Whose work is accomplished, their life-task o'er;
But for thee, have they left a harvest store
Of maxim and precept, and thought combined
With the varied research, ye term food for the mind,
Which should, like the body, in youth receive
    A nutriment solid and plain,
For time then lost, ye can never retrieve
    When memory fails to retain
All that it for expansion needs,
And only on lighter literature feeds;
And the similitude hence draw we,
In which both body and mind agree.

        Elementary education,
        Words of verbose compilation,

To the young imagination,
Meaning ofttimes trepidation,
Interspersed with castigation,
And occasional commendation.

But precedence in the classes
First we give to gentle lasses,
From whose ruby lips there runs,
The softer tone of Southern tongues;
While even those of harsher sound
Have grace from such sweet voices found;
And these blushing buds unfolding,
Fashioned fair in nature's moulding,
By skilled touch can here display
Other forms of earth and clay,
Which are beauteous made as they
Into subjects. Oh! how varied
May the mind of youth be carried!

But more than one of these already have been quoted,
When to music and to painting we our thoughts devoted,
And history and geography, twin sisters, we have noted;
But before proceeding further for information, I
Would ask wherefore abstruse subjects end in the letter "y"?
Be it that they each and all present
Questions perplexing, differing in intent,
Which to develop intellect are meant,
And when to solve their mysteries the learners oft may try
The vowel's sound again expressed asketh the reason "why?"
But this is merely theory—nor pause I for reply.

And now turn we for some brief space
From things which lend to life a grace,
To consider the skill which all untired
So perseveringly hath acquired
The triumph which spans the chasm wide
With a bridge of iron from side to side;
Whose giant frame with one vast stride,
Every impediment hath defied.
And 'tis alone the men who claim
From the mighty engine to take their name,
Whose discoveries thus by all averred
Have the greatest boon on mankind conferred.
Oh! worthy of honour such men I deem,
Who by the practical use of steam,
Have reduced the daily drag and toil
Not only of those who till the soil,
And stoutly thresh the harvest spoil;
But there are others who profit beside,
As much or more—though to them is denied
Expression's power—oh! difference wide!
Which must man from the animals ever divide.

Skilled nature, her work when 'twas begun,
Disdained to create the murmuring tongue;
And each his place by instinct fills,
Nor questions aught his Maker wills;
By man controlled—he but obeys
And serving spends his few short days.
For though without the gift of speech,

To man contentment he may teach
In the allotted sphere of each,
And society's members the most humane
Are those who diminish the sum of pain
For the creatures oppressed, who ne'er complain.

Of domestic economy men may boast,
But who are they who promote it most?
And who likewise facilitate business and pleasure
As the case may be, when moments of leisure,
With men are so few, that all are agreed
It is not the distance, but the speed,
By which they accomplish a journey at need.

And so after all 'tis the time they measure,
Which as time is gold, what marvel they treasure;
That which once spent, to refund is in vain,
And honour then surely, repeat I again,
It is meet that the skilled engineer should attain;
Who by the careful study of intellectual powers
Has made the little minutes do the work of hours.

   Merrily, merrily turns the wheel,
      And the wife to its murmur sings,
  Till years to her startled gaze reveal
      There's a "Jenny" that faster spins.
  Yet looks she not with a jealous eye
  At the maidens whose swift fingers ply,
  For 'tis steam which makes the shuttles fly,
      And her admiration wins.

Such, then, the force, the most akin to life,
Whose motive power, producing peace or strife,
To various aims is often thus devoted,
Too numerous in these verses to be quoted.
The torch of life enkindled, sets that life in motion;
So steam, of fire engendered, sendeth ships across the ocean.

Oh! marvellous concentration of force!
    By steam and machinery combined,
Calculated, 'tis said, by the power of the horse,
    Which by numerals vast is defined.
But stay! here a difficult question arises,
About which the wise may have many surmises;
For while all these horses by hundreds ye count,
'Tis the units, remember, that make the amount.
Now horses so vary in sinew and bone,
That the strength of each horse should be counted alone;
And then the statistics should likewise declare
The species and age of each horse entered there;
For otherwise 'twere altogether in vain
An adequate notion e'er to attain
Of the animal force that to steam ye compare,
Which, taken at hazard, I reckon unfair.

And so to arrive at a just computation,
Of the power of the engine for your information,
Let the speed per mile be ascertained,
As you calculate that of a racer trained,
And this to the locomotive applied

From station to station the time occupied,
Will at once the engine's power decide
And prove that the racers on fire that feed
For strength and endurance take the lead,
And no other with these can dare to compete,
Be they ever so powerful, ever so fleet.

Then time-measured distance, it must be confessed,
Appears the only accurate test
Of the wonders accomplished by means of steam,
Which, being a thoroughly practical theme,
These remarks are not misplaced, I deem.

Of a bygone invention next will I treat,
    A carriage without a body,
For between the wheels was the rider's seat,
    And he called it his horse and hobby.
That they with rapidity travelled 'tis true,
    And a noise in the world they made,
In a two-fold sense, but only a few
    Hobby horsemanship then displayed.

For then it took three wheels to do
The work accomplished now by two.
A quaint old saying still finds grace
Which likens anything out of place
To a wheel in excess of the number four,
Although no vehicle ever had more.
But in this case the number three
Seems one too many, as all agree.

And so 'twas reserved for the present age
To exhibit the subject in quite a new phase,
By a perfect machine, now all the rage,
Which for speed and lightness I'll engage
To eclipse the machines of former days.
Now the rider is seated above the wheel,
In the rear of which, viz., close at his heel,
Is another, smaller by a great deal.
Like a younger brother, by earnest zeal,
 It keeps up the pace
 In the unequal race,
 Following closely the track to trace.
Though the order of precedence here is reversed,
As 'tis commonly claimed by the little wheels first,
Like young school-boys to whom conceded
A privilege by their stature needed.

But to return to my self-imposed task,
A moment's attention again would I ask,
To point out the advantages which must accrue
To the bicycle riders, and these are not few;
Strength of muscle, and sinew, and nerve,
Such three-fold purpose it will serve;
And who can tell the delight they share
But those who speed through the sweet, fresh air.
Then wonder not that the bird, whose wing
Cleaveth that air, so loves to sing,
When instinct has taught them thus to tell
The happiness that all know well

Who feel the hidden power which lies
In the air, when naught 'twixt earth and skies
Is there to sully its sweet supplies.
And they who rise with the early sun
To travel onward till day be done,
Know that in the morning tide
Vital force and strength abide.

    And here allow me to deduce
    A remark for which I find excuse,
        In speaking of this invention;
    Which is, that in the good old times
    Were instituted roadway fines
        With doubtless good intention;
    And cunningly then the traveller turned,
    If he another route discerned,
        Avoiding such detention.

And a statute of rules for horses and mules,
While the asses were also named in the schedules;
By which, don't mistake me, I do not mean fools,
But the docile creature who patiently draws
His two wheels or four. And such the bye-laws
Made by those who supposed that none could elude
A toll levied strictly each class to include.
But at length there fleetly and noiselessly comes
A machine that ruthlessly through the Act runs,
And not only the Act but the turnpike through,
In right of exemption to all quite new;

For the bicycle makes itself free of the road,
Disregarding *in toto* the old-fashioned code,
Whose compilers, no doubt, had their share of abuse,
Until these same highways fell into disuse,
Locomotion becoming by other means greater,
Though perchance we shall see, either sooner or later,
That steam power and bicycles may vie together,
Though the latter are less independent of weather,
Inasmuch as the rider can't use an umbrella.

While travelling along in the sunshine or rain
It is somewhat perplexing to have to retain,
And by close calculation to tax the brain
With the mileage question, when prompters old
Information of every sort withhold,
And in ruin are crumbling in moss and mould.
Thus old Father Time has their faces concealed,
Which a mask of rude nettles and weeds may shield
From th' inquiring gaze of the passer-by,
Who looks with a disappointed eye
On the old milestone as he draweth nigh,
Whose figures he faileth to descry
On the form half hidden in mockery ;
But the tall finger-post with its outstretched arm
Seldom fails its mute greeting, in the East called "salaam,"
Which, both being silent, the comparison rendered,
Though novel, I trust may escape being censured.

Now it seems to me that a prospect appears
Of fresh need for these relics of former years.

Then mark all ye, who are overseers,
Make up your accounts, call in your arrears;
'Tis time more use should be derived
From roads at such great cost contrived,
And old institutions be revived.
For again as the swift four-in-hand dashes past
The horn of the guard blows a cheerful blast,
And whether in sunshine, or whether in rain,
These stony monitors still maintain
Their post as informers of distance and speed.
To compare with time passing is easy indeed,
Though the old village clock be not always agreed
With the time as in London, and slightly mislead
Those who their faith too implicitly place
On the index displayed by its honest, round face;
Forgetting the constant exposure which must
Be ever withstood—while the rain and the dust
Without strict attention its works would encrust
With a thick over-coating of so-called red rust.

But it surely affords some relief to dispense
With tables—which naming I mean no offence
To their author or student—though the latter in vain
Seeks from you, Mr. B., information to gain,
Too often, alas! when of steam-boat or train,
The times and the seasons so puzzle his brain,
That he fails in the estimate he would attain.
And as to conclusion this subject now draws,
I trust with success, I have pleaded my cause,

For the old institutions of times they call good,
Which, if duly considered, and well understood,
Ye would ne'er to oblivion their verdict pronounce
With jest and derision, which I would denounce.
But let every improvement be tested as such,
Before 'tis adopted and praised over-much.
Progression, know then, I've no wish to impede,
But surely so far we must each be agreed
To preserve all that's useful and add to the store,
Discoveries manifold yet more and more.

Now this train of thought following, I would direct
Your attention a few moments here to inspect
The carriages horseless—whose silent wheels stand,
As though waiting an unseen driver's command,
And if turns go by ages, the oldest comes first,
Although as a consequence, shabbiest and worst.

But oh! if that ancient body could tell
Of the bodies it carried, what to them befell,
Its panels might echo some secrets of State
Once breathed by Napoleon, still known as "the Great."
The thirst for ambition which naught could assuage
Is traced through his history in every page,
By that golden dream which onward him led
To the field where his soldiers' blood was shed.
Did he care for the suffering, or mourn for the dead?
Ah! no, the aspect his features wore
Endurance betokened and strength, which more

Resembled those emblems of France he bore—
The royal eagle on poisèd wing,
Who is of the feathered race a king;
And more majestic none than he
Who soars in his proud dignity!

But here an adage old, though not to be denied,
Has, to my thinking, been exemplified;
For pride destruction oft precedes,
And so the haughty spirit leads
To fell disaster born of evil deeds.

Ah! who is this that next in thought we view,
As fancy peoples yon barouche anew?
A monarch proud, whose life outlasts his sway—
'Twere wonder crushed ambition lived a day;
Nor e'en in that lone island dared the captive say
That here "I monarch am of all that I survey."

His territories gone, not one remained,
'Twas in some followers' hearts alone he reigned.

But stay! we are wandering all too long
Events of another age among.
Through the wheelèd ranks we now proceed
Whose style the ranks of fashion lead.
But the desideratum of lightness and strength
Claim to be dwelt upon at length;
And too well the noble horse doth know
Of the builders whose names in that vast row,

Which is most truly his friend or his foe.
Then look beyond the varnish and paint
And by inquiry thyself acquaint
With tyre and wheel, and pole and shaft.
See each be strong and light of draught.
For men who call themselves humane,
How few in this are free from blame.

And here would I make mention
Of a wonderful invention;
'Tis an omnibus gigantic
From across the broad Atlantic.
Such colossal importation
Would convey a population
All entire—if such their wish is,
Their abode to change, like gipsies.
On a smooth and level surface
Those thick wheels have ample purchase;
And their power throughout the distance,
Meets no atom of resistance.
Not a stone save when it hails
May remain upon its rails;
And horses when it is their lot
To work these cars with even trot,
Seldom seem oppressed or hot.

Then how cheerily sound the harness bells,
Whose peal the approach of the tram-car tells;
And retreating continue in long vibration,
Till, arrived at the journey's termination,

There occurs a scene of transformation,
Causing the horses a strange sensation,
When from the vehicle sundered, to find
The direction they're bound for changed like the wind,
And what was the forepart becomes the behind.
Nor does it lessen their mute surprise
To see that conveyance of ponderous size,
Which with no great effort they have conveyed
With only each other's united aid.

>Of the genus "amphibious" oft have we heard,
But 'tis something new to apply that word
To things inanimate, which a double
Purpose supply, and save much trouble;
For here is a body constructed to float,
Which when minus its wheels becomes a boat;
But if entire allowed to remain,
'Twill work on the roadway or country lane,
As well as 'twill on the glassy lake,
When from the wheels the body ye take.
Then let us picture some fair view,
And the joy of a summer picnic crew,
To whose wild chant the rocks reply
In echoes on the winds that die;
And many a youthful heart beats high,
As all too quick the moments fly,
While near the shore the rowers ply.
But when from out that boat ye land,
No matter whatsoe'er the band

To couple ye may now exist,
One moment to my secret list!
Fair maidens, then your names ye'll change;
Nay, blush not, though 'tis passing strange,
For all who in the boat with you
Have companied know that 'tis true
That ye and they were termed the crew,
When by transition quick performed,
To passengers ye are transformed.

But time fast speeds, nor longer may
We dwell on pictured youth's bright day,
But to our task. As ye advance,
Now sterner objects claim a glance,
And from the works which are in turn
Presented here, ye something learn.
For oh! how wide is the range of thought
Which subjects varied together have brought,
So that far and near, from sea and from land,
Ye may gather instruction where ye stand,
And miles of mental travel have we gone through together
Regarding not the seasons or rough and stormy weather.
I've carried thee to the wild man's home,
　　The wild man to behold;
But in the Antipodes alone
　　Have we their habits told,
Though there are many tribes of earth
More or less civilised by birth,
Who represented here, a comment claim.
Then stay not to recount each name,

Although did time permit, and we had likewise space,
Subjects of interest open out from every savage race,
Whom Nature aptly has designed for a distinctive place.
'Tis said that by her magic touch she makes the whole world kin,
And mystic is the power she holds thy sympathy to win.

    For beings such as some of these,
    From brutes removed but few degrees,
    Untutored, save by instinct solely,
    For life's demands providing only.
    What wonder, under such a master,
    If they should fail to progress faster.
    Then honour to the explorer bold,
    And when the world's chart is unrolled,
    See who can claim the greatest share
    Of honour for discoveries there.
    England, 'tis thine! for thou dost rule the wave,
    Which oft hath been thy heroes' briny grave;
    For whose sad fate Britannia sorely grieved,
    While honouring those whose enterprise achieved
    Discoveries great, by which her right extends
    To civilise all those whom she defends.
    And thus the progress of the world to aid
    Her sons earn laurels which can never fade.

    For chronicled arrangement would ye ask
    Of tribes and races? I forego the task,
    Referring you instead to that prose guide begun
    About the year of grace one, eight, and fifty-one.

The work was like a stripling then,
    For it was young and slender;
But books gain bulk as well as men,
And three years multiplied by ten
    More full account should render.
And as a man mature of age
By courtesy is counted sage,
Appeal we to each lettered page,
    The while our thanks we tender
To those from whom the record grew,
Which aids so much this brief review
Of subjects varied, old and new,
All which possess their histories true
    Of divers form and gender.

And this remark may be applied
To sculptor's skill, exemplified
    By forms of beauty moulded,
To charms bewitching that abide
    'Neath draped design enfolded;
And some whose features veiled betray
A modest smile, as if to say,
Gaze not too long, pass on thy way;
For graces thus in part concealed
Attract far more than if revealed.

A maxim which if laid to heart
By those who form the leading part
Of Fashion's world, as it should be,
'Twould raise the tone of society:

A remark I intend to apply to the ladies,
No matter whatever their age or their grade is,
Who'll deem me not, I trust, unkind,
Because I boldly speak my mind.

Now tell me, whence is the standard drawn;
Is the model of beauty yon graceful fawn?
If so it excludes the stately and grand,
The Minervas and Junos of classic land;
Then trace it at once to the only source,
No matter the form of its after course,
For beauty's perfection, I dare to insist,
Must first in the soul of the Poet exist;
'Tis there its silent influence woos,
The latent gift of his heavenly muse,
'Tis there that the image which imbues
Descriptive power with its rosy hues,
By reflection warms with the fire of life,
The spirit of song in his soul that's rife;
Which having the power of verse to express,
The painter and sculptor must freely confess;
While 'tis not given them to know
From whence their inspirations flow,
'Tis to the poet that much they owe
When they would indulge in those mythical flights
Which artists consider as their licensed rights,
Desiring, it seems, to make us well acquainted,
With those whom the world once believed to be sainted.
And surely 'tis fit that I introduce here
The saint who in armour is made to appear.

I allude to St. George, the green dragon who slew,
(What he did with it afterwards nobody knew)
Or whether his valour then somewhat abated,
Or with this success was he so much elated,
That the gauntlet for England as Champion he threw,
And into her patron saint then quickly grew.
But of the poor dragon we hear nothing more ;
Were there none of his kindred his death to deplore?
If so it would seem that we've lost all the traces
Of one of the most remarkable races.

And now the same legend goes on to relate
Why the Saint to the dragon shewed such deadly hate,
Which, like other romances, we find have one basis,
As a lady, 'tis said, oftentimes in the case is,
So it once came to pass, that in fear and dismay,
A royal princess saw crossing her way
A snake, or a dragon, call it which you may.
It resembled the creature that Eve once betrayed ;
What wonder her daughter then seemed so afraid.
Nor was the position altogether much mended
By her being so young, likewise quite unattended.
When in opportune moment the Saint-Knight advances,
In his hand poising one of those sharp-pointed lances
Called by some pikes, but by others a spear,
Although to the dragon it must have been clear
'Twas a turnpike to him, whose law was in force,
As it truly an obstacle proved to his course ;
Who not one step further had power to proceed,
But expired there and then ; with no one to heed

The struggle now over. Death ended the strife ;
But another arose, which threatened the life
Of the knight with captivity, if in the snare
Of Cupid he fall, and none bid him beware !
For the beast he had slain was a danger far less
Than the beauty in all her loveliness,
Who now draweth near, her thanks to proffer,
Although, perchance, had she known of the offer
Which her father the king had right royally made,
It might have required some power to persuade
The timid approach of this gentle maid.
When the dragon the debt of nature had paid,
On her side, at least, was the compact fulfilled.
'Twas no longer fear her bosom that thrilled ;
But if it is not so why then trembles she
Like a leaf of the pale mimosa tree ?
'Tis but admiration, she fondly thinks,
For a noble deed, but with mystical links
This same little Cupid we've mentioned above
Has encompassed her heart with the bondage of love.

    But St. George was bent on adventure bold,
    And yet too bright were his spurs of gold,
        At heart to entertain,
    The thought of a domestic life
    E'en with a princess for a wife ;
        And so 'twas all in vain
    That he had such high honour won
    Ere his career had scarce begun.

Alike in vain the pomp and pride
Of courts, and of a visioned bride,
To him who, wedded to his sword,
Had sworn that by his knightly word
    That age of chivalry
Should own him champion of the Cross,
Nought reckoning sacrifice or loss,
    Foremost of such to be.

With spirit free as winds of Heaven,
Behold him then the first of seven,
Fit champion of the British host
Who of a birthright free can boast.
And of that host I will maintain
St. George was foremost in the train

Of Britain's armèd band of four,
Whose Union name I here restore.
But incomplete our tale would be
Should I omit the other three,
Or fail to take note of the mysteries seen
By Scotland's St. Andrew, albeit I deem
That the spirits he met were an uncanny race,
And the ladies whom after he rescued in Thrace
(Who from swans into damsels he quickly transformed,
That is, if by hist'ry I'm rightly informed)
All loved him so dearly, that when he took leave
They followed him after, we're taught to believe ;
But whether successful or not the pursuit
Is a question on which the records are mute.

Be this as it may, the swift course of time
Him followed likewise, till when past his prime,
Resolved that his last years in Scotland he'd spend,
And that where he'd gained life, there life he would end.
So travelling back to the place of his birth,
He retires to a cave far away in the earth,
For the space of a year, for study and thought,
Until one day, alas! in secret was brought
The head of the Saint to the king for reward,
And more pitiless fate was perhaps never heard.

Next see from Hibernia a knight of renown,
St. Patrick, who hailed from famed Dublin town,
Who also on foreign adventure was bent,
When to Rhodes 'gainst the Turks and the pagans he went,
And who likewise fell in with the ladies of Thrace,
With whom he resolved every danger to face.
Then hereafter in Greece was the green knight enrolled
In the tournament lists as a champion bold,
Whose prowess so daunted that all were agreed,
As he came in their midst, that they would concede
All honour to him and his brave Irish steed.

Then a word for St. David, the Cambrian bold,
Who came by his death through exposure to cold
After hot-blooded conquest, when forward in pride
His followers he led, and fought by their side;
Who all, to distinguish them, wore a green leek,
Which seems to us rather a comical freak.

Be this as it may; the pagans' conceit
Was well taken out of them by a defeat;
For the champion of Wales knew how to contend
With the foes of the country he'd sworn to defend.
Then from France, Italy, and Spain
Three champion knights their honours gain,
St. Denis, Anthony, and James;
And though I but record their names,
'Tis from no mean appreciation
Of deeds which, by the revelation
To us preserved, should still incite
To courage in the cause of right;
And this true moral have we here,
Let life be less than country dear.

Over the wide expanse of earth,
Wherever genius hath its birth,
Each nation here is represented
With all they have with skill invented;
Some by innate science taught,
While others have by study sought
For that skill in art and science
Which sets boldly at defiance
Every obstacle or trial
Which may be, by self-denial,
Overcome. Oh! then could ye
But know the varied history
Of all that here is gathered in
A deeper interest some would win.

But here are lips without the tongue,
Cold, like a world without the sun ;
They lack the glow and power to tell
What words of admiration fell
From other lips that love to praise,
Interpreting their owner's gaze ;
And here the sculptured breast of snow
That can no heart-throb ever know,
Moulded by those who long ago
Dreamed of a beauty more than human,
Formed as an angel, loved as a woman.
And thus it is in fancied guise
The artist seeks to realise
Visions that sweet sleep unveils,
Which to describe expression fails.
For such things to the soul belong
As around in mystic throng,
While the wearied body slumbers,
They appear in countless numbers,
And to design the undertaking
That the artist on awaking
Gives a stamp of psychic birth
To stone or marble from the earth.
Mirth's sunshine it now resembles ;
Or a shadow almost trembles
In illusion o'er the brow,
Which ye pause to gaze on now.
Lofty thought is here presented,
There expression calm, contented,

Here a pensive smile befitting
Lovers' joys too often flitting.
Every care and every passion
Hence is shewn in some such fashion;
While 'tis sculpture ofttimes raises
Heathen myths of pagan ages
Known but in the classic pages;
And to these it gives a form
Calculated to adorn
Buildings which are dedicated
To Art, so oft with pleasure mated.
And such the building we have here,
Concerning which one point is clear,
That, being for the public good,
'Tis only justice that it should
Claim a right of full exemption
From all rates that we can mention,
One of which, long since repealed,
Would otherwise have here revealed
Statistics, certainly not small,
Had window tax been claimed at all.
And would I further yet dilate
On the amount in aggregate,
I think that if we were to trace
The same in any given space,
Why, the collector's calculation,
If subjected to computation,
And the returns were noted down,
Of many an influential town,

They'd here be found as quite exceeded
By those for pleasure only needed.

And now I think this goes to prove
That those were wise who did remove
All barriers to the observation
Of nature's beautiful creation,
Oft to cheerful thoughts impelling
When 'tis viewed within the dwelling;
For men and plants alike, we know,
In light and air best thrive and grow,
Which light and air their ingress gain
By means of the crystal window-pane.
And thus we come to realise
All the results we here comprise
In a place of such vast size;
Life and health from without admitted
Within an area of beauty, fitted
With every refinement that taste and skill
Can with science suggest the space to fill.
And thus to the mind is knowledge conveyed
By all that is aptly here displayed;
And while dreaming of pleasure alone, is acquired
Information that may have been long desired
By the student, who came with a view to pass
A long leisure day in the Palace of Glass;
Who here not only his strength recruits,
But goes home laden with mental fruits,
Cultured by others, to lessen the strain
Which study entails on the human brain;

That brain on which the pent-up soul
Presses severely when under control,
Of the myriad thoughts which therein crowd,
Like the locusts of Egypt in one dense cloud;
And the well-known expression of "power of brain"
Is oft misapplied and spoken in vain;
For the power they allude to, I take as a whole,
To emanate from the power of soul;
Which uses the brain to work its will
By diffusing knowledge for good or ill.
Like a time-worn servant, as years pass by,
The brain grows weaker and then will die;
But the soul grows stronger by lapse of time,
And none know when it attains its prime,
Whose course is advancement from life's dawning day
Without let or hindrance, defying decay.
And how perfect soever to thee may appear,
The attainments of genius now evidenced here,
Ye know not, ye guess not to what height sublime,
The soul when 'tis freed from the body may climb,
Unbounded by time, unbounded by space,
To roam all untrammelled o'er nature's broad face,
Where infinite knowledge enrolls her vast page
Of the soul's inexhaustible heritage.
And as breezes unseen fan the smouldering fire,
So life's torch of flame rises, higher and higher,
When received by the breath which was with that life given,
And which ne'er can be lost, but returneth to Heaven.
'Tis true that I named this a holiday tale,

But a high moral influence still should prevail.
Behold then here a space devoted
To subjects now with reverence quoted;
And tiny bannerets are placed
With each a text or maxim graced,
Emblems such as indicate
That the spot they decorate
Would proclaim how it rejoices
In its many lettered voices.
Heralds they of tidings true,
Addressed alike to me and you,
A vast store of wisdom to which you've access.
No matter whate'er be the creed you profess,
Or what be the language by you comprehended,
The freedom of study to all is extended,
To all! Yes, from North, South, East, or the West,
Who here may be drawn are protected as guest,
Where no order of priestcraft has power to molest.

But some there are who desire to persuade
By the senses, more than the heart, I'm afraid,
By rendering holy truths obscure.
Can such physicians hope to cure
A heart diseased? No! let the Word
In its integrity be heard;
And carried as a birthright free
To distant lands beyond the sea.
And England, thou mayst honoured be
When such a trust devolves on thee.

For surely love's persuasive power,
Like the silent dew on the tender flower,
Refreshes, nourishes, and gives
A joy to everything that lives;
And as those downy leaves expand
By nature's breath—from Heaven fanned;
See, each in its appointed place
Where fitted best that flower to grace.

'Tis thus that ev'ry leaf that blows,
And contributes a share to the fragrant rose,
To thee and to me can a moral disclose.
For truly if there is designed
By one Divine, all-ruling mind,
Component parts of mould exact
In nature's world—why then the fact
Follows, of course, that the order and sphere
Of each man is allotted here.

Now fitting 'twere that I recall,
An admonition to ye all,
Familiar—though long years have past;
'Tis this: that those in faith who cast
The bread of life on waters vast,
Shall in a while such gift regain,
In goodly store of golden grain.
Then would ye aid the gathering in
From the wild wastes of death and sin?
In faith, thy work at once begin.

And who are they the toil that share?
For now are the angel reapers there,
Who in mysterious power, unseen,
Over the world's wide acres glean.
No spot too distant for their flight,
No day too short, too black no night.

And those neglected ones, who lie,
Howe'er remote, they still descry;
And finding, bear away as prize,
To the soul's home beyond the skies.
And whether it be over mountain or sea,
'Tis the trackless path to eternity,
Where alone they can guide,
On the storm-clouds who ride,
Unheeding the rage of the fierce ocean-tide,
Whose billows hiss and roar as they sweep
O'er the tempest-tossed on the pitiless deep.
But there, even there, they a harvest reap,
Who ever their faithful vigil keep,
And though the ship be rent asunder,
With a crash o'er-powered by the deafening thunder,
Be sure that the troubled spirit can hear
Their sounds of welcome and glad good cheer,
For there never was scene of danger or war
But there the angel reapers are.

Now by the true-hearted 'tis always confest
That reality gives to religion a zest,

And to realise this, the end unseen
Of life's long journey, has ever been
The natural aim to which all would attain,
To whom then surely these words are not vain,
Although yoked with others of lighter strain ;
But one thing indestructible in nature there exists,
Which every form and phase of death with certainty resists :
It is the latent power in man known by the name of soul,
Which through his body permeates in one mysterious whole,
Whose members each with one accord
Obey the will of that unseen Lord.

    And when in the springtide of youth's glad day,
    To gaze down the vista of life's pathway
    Is to see but the flowers from hope that spring,
    Which in prospect the summer of life will bring ;
    And the vision has ever a rosy gleam
    To illumine the pathway of that day-dream.

    But summer arrives, with its toil and care,
    And thunder clouds shadow its pathway fair,
    While the current of life, with ceaseless flow,
    Ne'er stays for the dreamers who come and go ;

    Some the harvest fruit to receive,
    By industry bound in a golden sheave
    Of maxims remembered when life was young,
    Which by wisdom are taught and by poets are sung.
    And such reward in autumn they reap
    The talents of nature unburied who keep,

For the winter of life, so chill and drear,
That their influence pure may calm and cheer,
In the whispered accents of love's own power
Conveyed to the soul as a priceless dower.

Arrive they early, or tarry they late,
A welcome there is at the golden gate ;
And thither have thousands already sped
Borne away to the land of the so-called dead ;
But of these there are none, for the earth-life begun
Is but exchanged, when the gate is won,
For a life that is happy, and lovely, and pure,
Where the beauty of youth for aye shall endure ;
And the mind's capabilities fully expand,
To all that is noble, majestic and grand ;
While every enjoyment that intellect gives,
In the world of hereafter more perfectly lives.

Then gaze on it calmly, the prospect is real,
Nor long is the vista, whose end I reveal.

'Tis true that thorns obstruct the road
Of those who toil with weary load ;
But oft the gay, the glad sunshine,
Its beams across the path incline,
Smiling on every living thing,
As though it would be ever spring ;
Such nature's fruits are on the way,
Outspread within thy path to-day.
Accept the offering while you may.

And as yon bird of plumage bright
Beguiles with song his onward flight,
While upward borne on pinion light,
The mind in life's first opening years
That life depicts where naught appears,
Save that which most its life endears;
Ambition prompting to aspire,
Bird-like soaring ever higher,
This it is which bears thee on,
With thy faith within thee strong.

And if in thy manhood's breast
Faith remain chief honoured guest,
To whose allegiance thou art true,
As when the world was young and new,
Thy worst foes will be disarmed,
And happiness be there embalmed,
Though the source from which it grows
Only its possessor knows.

Here have we, then, the mystic power
Which courage yields in danger's hour.
Faith then points where duty leads;
But duty faith as consort needs.

Thus ye arrive another stage
Along the road from youth to age;
Which road has one resistless law,
That by each step ye nearer draw
To the end of that same road
Which should lead all to one abode.

What! though less firm and yet more slow,
Time's footprints in thy step may shew.
What! though the care and toil of years
A trace have left, which then appears
In every habit of the mind,
Which mighty wisdom has designed
To rest shall then be more inclined ;
For as the spirit o'er the body reigns,
And many an evil passion there restrains,
And all thy tasks allotted to fulfil
Are so dictated by this sovereign's will ;
What marvel, then, that those who long have served,
Claim for themselves a rest so well deserved,
And from sorrow and care to be
Exempt through all eternity.

Eternity ! 'tis no far distant spot,
That angels dwell in, and where men are not.
Nor is it beyond the azure sky
Veil'd by the clouds from thy human eye,
And where ye behold the starry spheres
That have canopied earth for countless years.

'Tis but the port when the voyage is o'er,
For which long since ye have left the shore,
And from whence ye will put to sea no more ;
The harbour of refuge for weary feet,
Where the stormy billows cease to beat,
And where the day has never a night,
For there is a tower that diffuseth light

Whose beams reflected ofttimes stray
From out the port, to guide the way
By the presence of hope, in a cheering ray;
And each crested wave of trouble past
By so much brings thee nearer the last,
And like the boat it drives to land,
Uplifts thee high upon the strand.

And the power that stilleth the angry wave
In many an unseen ocean cave,
While the tempests roar, and the storm fiends rave,
Is the same that willeth thyself to save.
For it dwells within thee a willing guest,
Like the dove of peace in her sheltering nest,
Above the storms of the earth finds rest.
Nor heeds the sound of the wintry leaves,
Which the wind is drifting beneath the eaves,
And who lieth secure and safe from harm,
Above the world, though amidst the storm.

And such the state of the mind at rest,
When 'tis by wisdom and truth possessed;
And such the gifts reflection gains,
When leisure for thought the mind obtains;
For meditation expands the mind
Above the millions of human kind;
For the limits of knowledge are undefined,
And extend beyond the trifling span
So sadly miscalled the *life* of man;

Whereas that life is but begun
When in this world its course is run ;
And it seems to depart like the setting sun,
Which sheds its radiance through other spheres,
When from thy vision it disappears ;
But the golden light it leaves behind,
Like the influence pure of a genial mind,
Is awhile reflected where it hath shined,
And though 'tis now by the heavens closed o'er,
It existeth still and for evermore ;
For the mortal tenement alone
On lease is let, to form a home
For the in-dwelling spirit, which must forsake
Its clay-built house, and upwards take
Its flight far away through limitless space,
Sustained by the power of that unseen grace
Whose presence concealed, as the seed when sown,
In the time of hereafter will be seen and known.

For the millions of flowers, that sleeping lie
In glory, shall bloom 'neath the summer sky,
And none, I trow, will then take heed
Concerning the fate of the parent seed,
Which will in its earth-bound tomb decay
While the flower is freed from the clods of clay.
And we know that the will of the great All-wise,
Decrees that thy soul, like that flower, shall rise
To dwell and to thrive in a genial clime,
When past are the days of the old earth-time ;

And the sheltering mansions love prepared
Will then by the human flowers be shared,
As each will bloom in the chosen place
Which love decides that they best will grace,
While the gifts and talents earth-life did bear
Will live in a higher culture there.

Like the wild flower born by the lone wayside
May become, transplanted, the garden's pride,
For by culture and care its charms expand
'Neath the eye and the touch of a master hand;
And it ne'er shall return to the place of its birth,
Where the thorns and the hemlock encumber the earth.
For these, when the mower comes to mow,
Will share one fate, as ye all must know.
And that through the world, not a distant spot
Shall be then passed over, by him forgot,
And destruction will follow where he doth lead,
As he clears the earth of the noxious weed,
While he gathers the flowers with careful hand,
For they're destined to bloom in the summer-land.

But time's warning finger bids us to return
From reverie, dreaming, and once more to learn
That though, like the flight of a bird in the air,
Our thoughts wander over this world so fair,
Yet 'tis well that we ever remember meanwhile
How stands our account with yon hard-faced dial,
Who under no circumstance ever will lend
Of time fresh supplies for that ye mis-spend;

But who, like a stern creditor, levies his taxes
On time as it passes, and never relaxes
One moment his duty the swift hours to mark ;
And to his report take heed, then, and hark !
While those solemn sounds on the ear that fall
In magical tones are announcing to all
The portion of life that already has vanished,
A thought that too many would wish could be banished;
The aged, whose retrospect dates further back
Than they have a care life's journey to track ;
The youthful, because they well know how true
'Tis that hours of enjoyment are only too few ;
And that each hour so spent seems as if 'twas in chase
Of the next that's to follow, which gives little grace
To that which succeeds it,—until quite expended
Is each sunny hour of a day too soon ended.
And oh! how many a hope and fear
In whispers breathed to a willing ear,
Have ofttimes been repeated here,
As the parting hour draws near.

We've discoursed of the fishes and also of birds
Then surely the honey-bee claims a few words ;
For I think that a higher intelligence moves
One, who each hour of a short life improves.

  And as that sunny life discloses
  Flow'ry paths with sweetest roses,

Not alone on pleasure bent
They fulfil their wise intent,
And contribute as agreed
To the general good and need
Of their tribe, whose busy hum
Ceases not, till day be done,

That there is strength in union we
   May learn, then, from the busy bee ;
Who may be in conclave seen
A ruler choosing in their Queen ;
For whom, when chosen, they prepare
A royal escort, who will share
Her guardianship with jealous care ;
Whose weapons are ready for unerring thrust;
Quick and sharp-pointed they never will rust.
And when she ventures forth abroad
Round her swarm the busy horde ;
Whose mission 'tis that they convey
Food to cheer her, on the way ;
Or perchance that royal band,
With their wings the air have fanned ;
As though in Oriental state,
Travels some Eastern potentate.

'Tis instinct has these laws contrived,
Wherefrom such order is derived ;
Each worker knows his fitting post,
And they who work are honoured most.

Not so the drone, whose life of ease,
Ranks him below his fellow bees;
Who little ceremony use
T'wards one condemned that life to lose;
And when the warfare is begun,
By numbers is he soon outdone;
For creatures of such idle race
In that bee-world there is no place,
Who then to exit are compelled,
And from the hive by force expelled.

Then is it not from such as these,
The happy, busy, honey-bees,
That nature has shewn in synonymous terms,
The maxim which man by experience learns.
For business and pleasure, where both are united,
The toil of the first, by the last is requited;
And governing bodies with divers decrees,
Should regulate nations by laws such as these
Referred to above as those of the bees.

There are many, perchance, who'll pronounce incomplete
A poetical essay forbearing to treat
Of everything here to the senses presented
Which nature, or science, or art hath invented;
Such attempt were a folly, unless by all
The book received, like a fresh snowball,
An impetus forward, as swift time flows,
While, matter still gathering, in size it grows;

And every new object which here is admitted
With description in verse would claim to be fitted;
And the critics might also our taste much offend
By styling this volume a tale without end.
Then why treat of some subjects and why others miss?
The answer I give by a question—'tis this :—
Go ask of the flowers why the honey-bee's kisses
On some are imprinted, while others he misses,
And you'll find that, hid in their depths, there lies
A store of wealth, which instinct descries,
And he rifles the treasure for purposes wise.

And so like the bee, in this garden of glass,
From subject to subject we carefully pass,
Imbibing our knowledge, so sweetened with pleasure,
That we feel not the burden of such gotten treasure;
And works that are useful we thus only choose
The mind to expand, and all others refuse,
Designed the hour passing alone to amuse.
And it is with such motive that I would retrace
The records extant of thine own British race;
For what theme of study can more fitting be
Than thy title to prove to the land ye hold free?

I speak not now of those who were the first lords of the soil—
The Britons, who in hot dispute their island home embroil;
For harassed by their northern foes,
Whose power extending nearer grows,
    Alliance they invite

From Englishmen, who o'er the sea
Like wave on wave came bold and free,
   To aid the cause of right.
Yes, bold and daring were the men who sailed from
    Sleswick's shore,
*And land as friends, where English feet had never trod
    before;
And as they leaped on Thanet's strand,
With bow and buckler, spear in hand,
Appeared outspreading o'er the land;
Of Englishmen the first armed band,
Destined hereafter to endow
That land where they are strangers now,
With English name of high repute,
Then yoked with Saxon and with Jute,
But to thine island home applied,
Which peerless stands, by none outvied,
In dignity aloof from all,
Surrounded by her briny wall.

    But when they viewed the isle so fair,
    All thoughts of friendship faded there;
    Resolved they then that none should share
    With them such spoils of conquest rare.
    Ambition's fire thus wildly burned
    And friends to foes were quickly turned,
    When with the rage of deadly hate
    The Britons see, when 'tis too late,

    " A.D. 450.

Their dread, inevitable fate,
As well 'twere to attempt to stay
A mountain torrent on its way,
Or the angry waves advancing
Whose white horses, leaping, prancing,
Fill the thinking soul with wonder
Whence comes then that voice of thunder?
Are there beneath the waves concealed
Hosts by Neptune ne'er revealed?
Who, when they together strive,
All this tumult vast contrive,
And though the conflict's storm be o'er,
Sink—but to arise once more!

And such the hosts who nearer draw
In their might of martial law,
United in one fixed intent
To subjugate the men of Kent;
Spear in hand, or strong bow bent,
Oft resisting—oft pursuing,
And the combat oft renewing.

But cautious, shun those fortress towers
Whence British arrows fly in showers;
And Rochester in safety past,
Although by no means 'twas the last
Of their strongholds beneath whose power
Even the bold invaders cower;
And which for twoscore years and ten
Was guarded well by Kentish men.

Oh, could old Richborough's roofless wall,
The scenes of long past years recall,
It had echoed the sound of the wavy deep
As it thundered against its ancient keep.
But the waves that now find ingress there,
And gently bend to the summer air,
Are those which a golden harvest yield,
And the fortress transformed is a fruitful field.

We know that in those early days
They boasted not of roads or ways,
Nor charts there were, nor draughtsmen there
The line of march to then prepare.
But there beneath its leafy screen
Of sloping woods, e'en then was seen
Like band of crystal, fringed with green,
The Medway river in its course
Defying that invading force;
And sheltered by the wild wood shade,
The Britons there a camp had made ;
But ere the English rule began,
Or men of genius learned to span
With yonder arch of stone so wide
The swift, the ever flowing tide,
'Twas Aylesford termed and aptly so
As we will now proceed to shew,
By the bed of the river that lies below.

For not in vain the conquerors sought
A foothold firm as they onward fought,

Then midst shouting and tumult the hollow blows rattle
As though creatures amphibious were waging the battle;
And such were surely that English band,
Who could fight in the water, as well as on land,
Until with success, they carried the ford;
* Then Aylesford owned an English lord.
Thus Hengist gained Kent's master key,
And others must subservient be,
But there remains one enemy,
Who soon has felled the conqueror low,
And deals alike to friend and foe
The pointed shaft of his deadly blow.

  For Hengist mourns a brother slain,
  The noblest born of all his train;
  But short the wailing o'er the dead,
  And short the prayer at parting said.
  A few rough stones alone define
  The place of his uncoffined shrine,
  And those now termed the rank and file,
  With nobles rest 'neath that rude pile.

  Oh! victory's price was dearly paid
  By him whom brotherless it made,
  As general he alone must lead,
  With none to counsel act or deed.

* A.D. 455.

But time forbids that we should trace,
Each record of that princely race ;
Or how the soil by valour won,
Descends from father unto son ;
And who as Englishmen retain,
Their right o'er fertile Kent to reign.
Until as swift years pass away,
Still more extended grows their sway ;
And then from Essex marshy land
To where the Severn's river strand
Old Ocean meets with open mouth;
As from Sussex in the south,
Upward to the Firth of Forth,
England's boundary in the North,
Was governed by a line of kings
To whose review now history brings
Us to the point whence we digressed ;
Somewhat detaining here our guest,
Who, gazing on this noble screen,
Dwells on the changes that have been ;
* Since seven crowns held each a share
Of this our realm of England fair,

---

* Cantia or Kent, founded A D., 475
South Saxony ,,   490
West Saxony ,,   519
East Saxony ,,   527
Northumbria ,,   547
East Anglia ,,   575
Mercia ,,   582

And seven kingdoms were assigned
With limits clear to each defined,
But all united to withstand
The depredations on their land
Wrought by great Arthur, King of Wales,
Who, though it little now avails,
A certain poet oft assails;
Discoursing, in a sort of fable,
Of belted Knights of the Round Table,
Whose fame for ages has descended
To those whose country they defended.
'Tis thus that two-score men and four,
For such their number, not one more,
E'en in this our later age
Still inspire the poet's page,
And immortal valour claims
For all who bear such honoured names,
Records time cannot efface.
So we their gallant deeds retrace,
And honour give where such is due
To each bold-hearted knight and true.

But stay we not at length to scan
The episodes which now began,
And when amidst internal broils
Ambition urging war's turmoils,
Seven great sovereignties involved,
* Into one kingdom were resolved.

---

* A.D. 828.

Nor will I e'en apostrophise
Those of whom we but surmise
That these their busts in height or size
Resembled them in any wise.
For if the king of Mercia and of Wessex,
And those of Anglia, Northumbria, and Essex,
With Kent and Saxony could now behold
Themselves, I doubt not they would need be told
By what means to identify
Those who here their place supply,
And represent the Heptarchy.

But after years tend to combine
Under one crown the Saxon line,
And the forefather of thy monarchs proud
Was Egbert, who with learning was endowed;
Of mighty Charlemagne the chosen friend,
Who to no potentate did ever bend,
And Emperor of the West was termed,
Albeit, then, that none discerned
The hemisphere so-called, beyond the Atlantic wave,
And which, in after years, to man a new world gave.

But a thousand years their course have run,
Since the deeds of which I write were done.
A thousand years! why such may be,
Like a drop in the deep, the fathomless sea,
The ocean of eternity.

> But to return to Egbert's rule and reign,
> So oft disturbed by the aggressive Dane,
> That 'twould a marvel seem to be
> How war and study could agree.

And surely he deserves a comment of some length.
The first who did unite old England's future strength;
At Winchester he donned that comprehensive crown,
Which the mandate stern of death alone compelled him to lay down;
And with it passed a legacy of rapine, fire, and sword,
*To Ethelwulf, his first-born, but the second over-lord
Of England, whom the Northmen strove in vain to overthrow,
Than whom the English monarch had no more deadly foe.

> On pilgrimage to Rome he went,
> I trow with many a wise intent;
> St. Swithin bore him companie,
> And saintlier guide there mote not be.
> Each of his Royal children four
> In turn the crown of England wore.

> †The first was Ethelbald, whose reign
> May only passing notice claim;
> ‡And Ethelbert a few years more
> Spent in defending Thanet's shore,
> As history's records say, in vain,
> From the ambitious, conquering Dane.

---

* A.D., 837.   † A.D. 857.   ‡ A.D. 860.

And next there to the throne ascends
*Bold Ethelred, who well defends
That throne upheld in battles nine,
Befitting king of Saxon line.

Until at length, the struggle o'er,
The last of all the brothers four,
　†Alfred, the great of mind,
As England's monarch claim'd to be
Champion alike on land and sea;
　The first who thus combined
By use of so-called common sense,
A double method of defence.
And England's giant walls of wood,
　Armed with the iron prow,
Like floating forts their home defend,
　As the armour-plated now;
And wheresoever most the need
Thither with sail and oars they speed,
And confidence they lend
To those who garrison the shore,
And deadly hail of arrows pour,
With shouts re-echoed o'er and o'er,
Heard far above the billow's roar;
For many a sea-coast fort and tower
E'en then was raised by Alfred's power.

---

* A.D. 866.　　　　† A.D. 871.

Alfred ! as statesman, scholar, soldier, equally renowned,
As in the gentler arts the music of sweet sound,
Which served his purpose well, as harper in disguise,
When fearless to the Danish camp the monarch-minstrel hies.
Like as in Eastern lands they charm,
The reptiles bent on deadly harm.

Oh ! were it given me to write old England's history true,
I long would dwell on Alfred's reign, for reason's light it threw,
On those decrees, his wisdom named,
And to which he obedience claimed ;
Wisdom, learning, courage, all in one mind blended ;
'Twere pity that such gifts with Alfred's life were ended ;
For had the love of peaceful arts to his royal son descended,
The crown, for which so long in vain bold Ethelwald contended,
*To Edward the Elder had then been secured,
On a basis more lasting, which might have endured
All through the reign of Athelstan,
    Who next came in succession,
From whom again th' attacking Dane
    Strives to obtain possession,
Until by mighty effort strong,
Though all the night, in battle long,
The Saxon host have gained the day,
And freed themselves from Danish sway.

* A.D. 901.

What boots it, if again they strive
Who through that dreadful fight survive?
A Saxon king still rules the State;
* 'Tis Edmund now, whose cruel fate
Was dealt by murderous hand;
And as the hour-glass' ebbing sand
    Through one small outlet wastes,
So by the dagger's deadly brand
    Away the spirit hastes.
†And Edred gains, in right of years,
A crown which somewhat strange appears.
By which we mean no disrespect,
But heirs there were in line direct
    Of England's murdered King—
While Edred, lacking power of mind
In union Church and State to bind,
Was ruled, where had he ruler been,
As in the sequel will be seen,
The foul abuses then allowed,
Obscuring history like a cloud,
    Which to its records cling,
Never had occupied the page
With details of vindictive rage,
Which sullied then the name of priest
With direful sin, expected least
From those who bear such name.

---

* A.D. 941.   † A.D. 946.

Oh! hapless royal brothers twain
*Edwey, priest-ridden, whose short reign
Bears of Elgiva's blood the stain;
His innocent, his gentle spouse,
To whom no joy the Church allows,
Ascribing it a deadly sin,
To wed with one of cousin kin.

And sad the tale we here disclose
Of beauty and of beauty's woes;
For she whom Heaven had made so fair
With grace the English crown to share,
A victim fell to craft and scheme,
Though she could homage claim as queen.

O England, who could thus endow
Thy priests with power, I charge you now
Beware of those who joys domestic would oppose;
Not friends of Heaven are they, but foes.

'Tis passing strange that such relentless fate
As Edwey met, stirred not the deadly hate
    In his young brother's breast;
But Edgar, judgment lacking, as it seems,
Also for guidance on St. Dunstan leans,
    And yields to his behest,
Who on him in return such wily praise bestows,
As will the favour of the King towards him best dispose.

---

* A.D. 955.

*And Edgar, then, the peaceable, so by historians termed,
At such a price thy title was far too dearly earned;
And when by death's resistless mandate called away,
Thy second spouse, Elfrida, for her son usurps the sway;
†Wherefore the martyred Edward, her king and stepson, falls,
By her own order slain beneath Corfe Castle's walls.
Thus her ambitious wish she gains,
‡And Ethelred, her son, now reigns.
But retribution, not with footstep slow,
O'ertakes her now, and England's ancient foe,
Th' aggressive Dane, threatens to overthrow
The crown which had been gained at cost of so much woe.
But alas! th'unready monarch no foresight brought to bear,
And of the country's honour entrusted to his care
§He thought not when he ransomed her as from a captive's fate,
Forgetting that old England was an independent State.

But all too short the respite acquired by such a bribe,
And all too long the conflict for us to here describe;
Until at length bold Edmund, surnamèd Ironsides,
With valour and with wisdom the sovereignty divides
‖With King Canute, who quickly the sole dominion gained,
For 'twas but for a few short days that they together reigned,
When death, which sunders every social tie,
Struck with unerring blow his Saxon Majesty.

---

* A.D. 957.   † A.D. 975.   ‡ A.D. 978.
§ Danegelt, a tax paid to the Danes of £66 000.   ‖ A.D. 1015.

And next the royal Danish line
In three successions we define;
Canute the Great, whose diplomatic skill
Governed both Dane and Saxon at his will.
And they, united for the common weal,
Each for the country's good felt equal zeal;
Until, at length, with his forefathers laid,
Division of the kingdom had once more to be made,
To save it from the foul disgrace of strife and civil war,
A thousand fold augmented when th' opponents brethren are.

*For Harold all too quickly seized his absent brother's rights,
While Godwin and the nobles to treason he incites;
As the Harefoot, from his swiftness, was the first King Harold known,
But swiftly too, o'er ta'en by death, left vacant was his throne.

† Then came Canute the Hardy, whose pardon I must crave,
While censure from historians at once I fairly brave;
Because those long four syllables suit not my measured rhyme
And why such name his sponsors chose I cannot now opine,
Then two short years of violence, and tyranny, and crime,
And ne'er to be renewed again—here ends the *Danish line*.
‡A Saxon prince is then recalled from yonder Norman shore,
In whom they hoped the Saxon line to lastingly restore;
But favourites of other days their claim on Edward press,
Who while they courted him the more, the Saxons loved him less,

---

* A.D. 1036.   † A.D. 1039.   ‡ A.D. 1041.

And never in their hearts he reigned,
Although the rule he long maintained.

Yet has he left us one redeeming sign,
Fit offspring of the soul of man divine;
Whose instinct ofttimes leads him to revere,
A higher Majesty than those we gaze on here;
And he who Westminster an abbey named,
Has thus become 'mongst his successors famed.

Shrine of the mighty dead, what changes hast thou known!
A veteran of ages, standing thus alone,
In solemn witness of that early day,
When first uprose thy lofty turrets grey.
Religious zeal, pretended, was then made the fair excuse
Whereby his married life became a subject of abuse,
And wherefore then he wedded Earl Godwin's daughter fair,
'Twas but a hollow dignity that she his throne might share,
Who was as wife neglected, although gentle, true, and good,
Bearing her heart's deep bitterness alone as best she could.
And why the royal mother, to whom he owed his life,
Was likewise made a victim in his domestic strife,
In monkish cell to be immured, although advanced in age,
I never can be made to think for her a proper cage.

Such the infamous sins caused by one who confessed,
As we're led to believe, every time he transgressed.
But although 'tis no purpose of ours to defame
A life which concerns us now only in name,

Yet I cannot refrain a remark by the way,
Inasmuch as the world that ye live in to-day
Has professors of fair speech, as once it had then,
Who confessors are likewise. There *may* be such men,
But not one in a thousand, I trust, nor in ten.
At length, when Edward's reign its course had almost run,
As traveller homeward hastening views the setting sun,

  Knowing his journey to be near an end,
  And looks around for kindred or for friend
  On whose integrity he can depend,
  In some such train of thought reflected then the King,
  And sent a messenger his brother's son to bring,
  * Who outlaw once, on whom his country frowned,
  As freeman now sets foot on English ground.
  His royal uncle's summons scarce had he obeyed,
  When by another summons were his footsteps stayed,
  And this his native land, on which he trod,
  But yielded him a dwelling 'neath the sod.

  Checkmated thus was the Confessor's plan,
  But, baffled not, fresh tactics he began.
  The orphan Edgar, child of tender age,
  Was all too young in combat to engage
  Against the Dane, his country's ancient foe,
  Who rule so weak would quickly overthrow.

---

        * Edward the Outlaw.

But wiser counsels came to Edward's aid
As proved hereafter by the choice he made,
Whose kinsman William chosen to succeed,
By nature fitted was to rule and lead.

And who can best the honoured trust fulfil
To carry news of this, his sovereign's will?
None less than prince of royal blood is he;
The bearer of a nation's destiny.

For Harold, Godwin's son, the message bears,
Who then to William solemn fealty swears,
With promises the latter to assist,
But had he sworn in all points to resist
The Norman power, his oath, or vow forsooth,
    At least had had one merit—that of truth.

Perjured it seems by deed as well as word,
He thus the censure of the Pope incurred,
To whom already William had appealed
For judgment in the cause he then revealed.
And when the Pope for his encouragement,
A consecrated banner straightway sent,
A blessing bearing, which was then supposed
To be somewhere within its folds enclosed,
Likewise a ring, and relic still more rare,
A veritable lock of good St. Peter's hair.
But whether on that reverend head it grew,
Though we may doubt, I hope the Pontiff knew.

But Godwin, banished Earl, at length returned,*
Whose son, ambitious Harold, then discerned,
That by his mother royally allied
His was a claim that should not be denied;
And England's crown owns one more Saxon king,
By whom it was usurped from Edgar Atheling.

Not long did he such ill-got gain possess,
Not long exult in his supposed success;
For Norman William to the throne successor
Had been already named by Edward the Confessor;
And boldly to assert that claim,
Becomes his purpose and his aim,
Awhile the policy he tries
Is stratagem and prompt surprise,
For which he needs must gain allies;
Such were from Norway brought to fight
At Stamford for the Norman right,
And though the victory they lost,
'Twas soon revenged at priceless cost.

For oh! how little Harold guessed,
When he the Northmen hotly pressed,
No moment for repose or rest
Would to his troubled soul be given,
Unless that rest be found in Heaven.

* A.D. 1053.

How time was measured in those days
I'm not aware that history says;
But since its course commenced to run
'Twas e'er divided by the sun,
And when it twenty times had passed
Away from out the heavens vast,
And twenty times had risen again
In glory o'er the restless main,
On that blue main's high-crested wave
Was borne an army strong and brave,
And Harold, victor in the North,
Then hastes to meet them in his wrath,
A stern invader, sternly met,
A dire, a fatal fight beget.

But 'tis not here I would describe
The scenes when men together strive,
Suffice to say, the Saxon host
Bravely defended England's coast,
And to no mortal foe Harold the King did yield,
*Until he life and crown resigned on Senlac's fatal field.

'Twas then victorious William, received with loud applause,
Commenced the rule of England with a code of Norman laws,
So famed for moderation and judgment so discreet,
Not e'en the very Saxons felt oppressed by their defeat.
Until a visit to his Norman home is planned,
From whence when he returned, on nobles of that land,

---

* The Battle of Hastings, A.D. 1066.

The Saxons' wealth and their estates he lavishly bestows,
Thus raising cause of discontent among his former foes,
Who, in the struggle which too soon ensued,
Embroiled became in hopeless, deadly feud
Against a ruler, in whose spirit dwelt
The hardihood of Norseman and of Celt.

General he was, who every trial shared,
And every danger with his soldiers dared,
For to the North his Norman host he led,
Until with Tay's broad river out before him spread,
He sworn allegiance claimed from Scotland's crownèd head.

    'Twas then that he the Conqueror's title earned,
    As all who him opposed too dearly learned,
    Nor earl, nor baron dared his power resist,
    For well they knew he wisely would insist
    On feudal law with all its dues and rights,
    Which by an oath had bound them, as true knights,
    When summoned, to obey their sovereign's call,
    And rally to his standard, one and all.

    * Then Malcolm's army, all in vain,
    Once more oppose the Norman's reign;
    But as a means to end the strife,
    Atheling is pensioned off for life.

    Yet still it seemed the Conqueror's fate
    Never in peace to rule the State;

---

* A.D. 1071.

When trusted nobles round his throne
Conspired his title to disown,
And warned by Saxon lips alone,
He checked the seeds by mischief sown.

But turbulent and angry feud
Next in his family ensued,
And such rebellion who can smother
When 'tis brother wars with brother?

For jealousy the fire of passion feeds,
And peace destroys by its own evil deeds,
As in the sequel we proceed to shew;
For when by death the Conqueror was laid low,
The second William, and the second son
Of him who first the Saxon throne had won,
His brother's dukedom and his birthright gains,
But, Jacob-like, gets punished for his pains.
*The name of Rufus, chroniclers have said
His hair gained for him; 'twas what some call "red,"
And like his temper fiery, as we're told,
In all the deeds that his short reign unfold.

But architecture in his time, it seems,
Made some advances in gigantic schemes;
The Tower of London then was made complete,
And unlike modern building, square, or street,

---

* A.D. 1087.

Its name retains, though there be other towers
Where modern clocks reveal the passing hours,
Which each in turn old " Father Time " devours ;
And yet they represent him spare and slim
Holding a glass but half-filled towards the brim.

And had such custom common been to all,
Who dined as guests in Westminster's vast hall,
It might have saved the Red King's royal fame,
From a degrading vice now coupled with his name.

We read of thousands at his banquets fed,
For whom to take a contract by the head
Would have required the means of calculation,
Which then was rare in business or vocation.

There is a tract of land on Hampshire's shore
They call a Forest New, but surely more,
Fitting it where that forest old to call,
Which, seven long centuries past, saw Rufus fall !
A rugged cross now marks the tragic spot
Where he, as victim of an arrow shot,
Was target made for craven regicide.
The fact stands thus, and cannot be denied.

Not so, the statement that the younger son
Of Norman William saw the foul deed done,
Nor tarried to avenge it, or to see
His brother's corse disposed of fittingly.

Had such his conduct been established fact,
* And Henry's rule commenced by such base act,
Not all his learning, by which he became
In after years as Beauclerc known to fame,
Had e'er entitled him to honour and respect,
Which he as England's ruler surely might expect.
Awhile the Saxon wrongs were now redressed,
Who for some fifty years had been oppressed,
Until a daughter of the Atheling race
With wisdom he selects the throne to grace ;
And mighty was the union on that marriage day
Which bound two hostile nations 'neath King Henry's sway.

Who in such strength Duke Robert's claim resisted
When he returned, and on his rights insisted
By such stern argument admitting no reply,
But Henry's rule and crown intended to defy.
Norman and Saxon face to face then stood,
As brothers there opposed—their leaders of one blood.
But neither durst be foremost the contest to begin,
Although the sole dominion they each desired to win,
Till at length the Bishop Anselm arranged the terms of peace,
And dissensions for a season were then allowed to cease.

But when the Duke returned to his own Norman shore,
Conditions of the treaty regarded were no more
By Henry,—which, when Robert knew,
He strove the contest to renew.

---

* A.D. 1100.

But vain it were to follow the struggles that took place,
Or each event recorded in poetry to trace.
With Henry Beauclerc only it is we have to do,
And of the great ambition in his kingly heart that grew.
But the hope so dearly cherished that the Atheling should succeed
How vain proved in the sequel by disaster great indeed!
For when the fleet of Henry from Normandy set sail,
One failed to keep in company, so runs the tragic tale,
And that "delays are dangerous," as some with wisdom say,
Never was more completely proved than on their homeward way.
With reckless haste that truant ship, with her right royal freight,
Rushed onwards with all sails outspread to her impending fate,
  Which Henry's son, the Saxon's heir,
  Alas! too soon was doomed to share.
    But hark! what is that hollow sound?
    While like some headstrong fettered hound,
    Her keel up springs with sudden bound,
      As she for freedom strives.
    Another moment and her bow
    Plunges beneath the abyss below,
      And soon her frame divides;
    But not before a trusty band
    Of sailors there a boat had manned,
    Into which with haste and dread
    The Prince is hurried, as 'tis said,
    With some young nobles of his train;
    Who, led by hope—alas! in vain,

Had thought the shore they could regain;
When, high above the billows' roar,
Or the hissing sound as they downward pour,
On the deck while sweeping o'er and o'er,
Is heard the plaint of piteous cries,
Piercing as though to rend the skies,
That they may ope—to the souls that rise.
When on the luckless Atheling's ear,
Shrieks from his tender *sister* dear,*
    Impel a prompt return.
At once the royal command was given,
'Gainst which 'twere fruitless to have striven,
The end though they discern.
And so the edict was obeyed.
Awhile by tossing billows swayed,
That frail boat to the ship draws nigh,
And all on board for life will try,
Though all must know they're doomed to die.
A headlong plunge, and it was o'er;
Then sinks the boat to rise no more.
And England's hope has perished there,
With nobles young and ladies fair,
Who all the same sad fate did share;
And of all those who left the shore
But one set foot thereon once more,
Who the sad tale of horror bore.

---

* The Countess de Perche.

Ill news, they say, is fleet of wing,
For now the electric wire can bring
Its messages of joy or woe
Swifter than arrow from the bow.
But when the first King Henry reigned
No such discov'ry had been gained,
And thus from him they long concealed
The white ship's fate, which, when revealed,
'Twas as though that ponderous blow
The Beauclerc's mind would overthrow,
Who senseless fell, and, as 'tis said,
A sudden gloom his face o'erspread,
Which rested there till death released
Him by a too abundant feast.
But was it lampreys (that's the question)
Alone destroyed the royal digestion?
And if a jury on the body sat,
A stranger verdict none could find than that.

*Stephen the first, of Norman line the last,
Whose likeness here 'mong England's monarchs cast,
Manly his bearing, muscular his frame,
Asserting boldly to the throne his claim,
Awhile contentions marked his troublous reign.
Lenient and just towards those who did him wrong,
And mentally as great, as physically strong,
As one need be whose crown so long contested,
Was by the late King's daughter from its owner wrested!

* A.D. 1135.

But while exulting in the victory won,
Ere yet her triumph scarcely had begun,
Maude with success became so much elated,
That by all classes soon her name was hated,
And her quick flight from London was necessitated.
The captive King, released, then re-ascended
The throne, for which to hold he still contended,
In strife that only with his reign was ended.

*And here we welcome back the Saxon race,
And in their representative we trace
How from a sprig of broom upon the helmet worn,
His father gained the surname, now by Henry borne,
Who England's crown obtained by right of his descent,
And sought by every means he could the Saxons to content;
†And one of whom as chancellor he chose,
Who quickly in his sovereign's favour grows,
And such his numerous and gorgeous train
To vie with him it surely were but vain;
Until at length fresh honours on him laid,
Changed was the man by changed position made;
And as there is no pride so great
As that which apes a lowly state,
So Becket, who is styled a saint,
By ostentation of restraint,
Incurred his royal master's hate;
And thus provoked his cruel fate.

---

* A.D. 1145.   † Thomas à Becket, Archbishop of Canterbury.

Then history tells of penance made,
When in his massive tomb was laid
The King's once favourite; while remorse
Evinced by feeling somewhat coarse,
Induces Henry to submit
* With scourges to be sorely smit;
Esteeming this of means the best,
For his poor conscience to gain rest;
Without which no man, high or low,
One moment's happiness can know.

But after years all failed to bring,
Domestic peace to England's King;
While those whom he had deemed allies
Now each in turn his power defies,
And Scotland's monarch captive then †
Was made by some four hundred men;
Which tidings when in France were told
It seems that King was likewise "sold."
Now this expression, I'm aware,
Although 'tis one by no means rare,
By other meaning is defined,
And has no lawful place assigned,
Save in the sense of compensation,
By means of abstruse calculation;
And my remark were briefly stated
By saying that it then seemed fated

---

* Henry II. did penance at Becket's tomb, July 12th, 1174.
† A.D. 1174.

The King of France should be checkmated,
While he of Scotland fealty swears
To him the English crown who wears ;
And binding was that solemn oath
On him and his successors both.

But soon from out the east there flew
Tidings which consternation threw,
And like a lurid fire-brand flew,
   Which to revenge incites
The chivalrous, the good, and true,
   Whom we call Christian knights ;
Of whom the foremost leader was of England's crown the heir,
Prince Richard of the Lion Heart, who fired with zeal did share
In every danger that his knights were then resolved to dare.
Undaunted courage ruled a heart by nature not unkind,
And Richard, though of purpose strong, was generous of mind.

* But when as monarch he became.
A guardian of the English name,
He bartered for heroic fame
The fealty he had right to claim,
And Scotland's King has bought for gold
That which 'tis marvel could be sold ;
While royal estates, which with the crown
For ages had been handed down,

---

* A.D. 1189.

Were sacrificed for that great cause
In history known as holy wars ;
And Richard as an absentee,
His people's guardian failed to be,
And there was many an outlawed band
Claimed might as right throughout the land.

Meanwhile the King success attained,
And soon a champion's name he gained ;
And his career was scarce begun
Ere he a bride had likewise won,
Who, though as England's Queen we own,
Yet never graced she England's throne.
Were it my purpose to relate,
In due chronology and date,
The victories that Richard gained,
For which in after ages famed
As Cœur de Lion he was known,
And such a title he alone
Of all thy kings can justly own,
But though on this account his claim
That we record his deeds of fame,
Is surely strong, yet as our aim
Is time expended to improve,
Why on, like time, then must we move,
For tale of battles and of truce
Long past can serve no present use ;

An observation which applies
To subsequent events likewise,

When shipwrecked Richard in disguise,
Concealment as a pilgrim tries,
* And by a ring was he betrayed—
A costly ornament, 'twas said—
Offered as guerdon, or reward
For kingly shelter, bed and board.

'Tis passing strange that such small token
As that of which above I've spoken
Oft has the happiness betrayed
Of high and low of every grade ;
As witnesseth the luckless maid,
Who, like this lion-hearted King,
Her freedom forfeits through a ring.

But to return to Richard's fate :
Deprived of all his kingly state,
E'en then his lion heart was great,
And stood his friend when more the need
Than in the flush of valour's deed ;
And when his cause he had to plead,
And none there were to intercede,
Courage and truth so ably spoke,
And caused his captors to revoke
Their sentence stern—and whose decision
Was made, but with one wise provision,
That for the lion heart set free
To pay his subjects must agree

---

* White's History of England.

A pretty tolerable score ;
Some hundred thousand marks and more.*
Forthwith a tax on all was laid,
And willingly that tax was paid ;
And Richard's welcome by the crowd,
So justly of their monarch proud,
Was not unworthy, I'll engage,
Of that or any other age.
A twice crowned king ! 'twere pity he,
The people's guardian failed to be.

But 'gainst King Philip, once his friend,
He needs must Normandy defend ;
Where four long years in arms he stayed,
Which left no time for the Crusade
That, nothing, daunted, he had planned.
But never in the Holy Land
Destined again to take command,
Richard in Normandy was slain,
And there his lion heart was lain.

For thrice one hundred years, as we've already seen,
'Twixt Normandy and England a union there had been.
Now when a title and estates from age to age descend,
'Tis matter of a rightful pride these honours to extend,
And for possession undisturbed to manfully contend.
But here, in France, a province which for beauty none exceed,
From England's crown has passed away by reason of a deed

---

* £400,000 present value.

Against which every feeling of nature must recoil,
And which filled the Norman people with horror and turmoil.
Barbarity in ignorance may sometimes find excuse,
But John could no such claim assert, as shelter from abuse,
And, all agreed, deservèd well
The loss of power that him befell.

'Midst many a scene of cruel wrong,
With no desire to linger long,
Review we, then, the life of John,*
The only king who bore that name,
But which in after years became
The most familiar appellation.
Applied to this thine island nation,
And joined with one to represent
Both strength and power that sure was meant,
When what was termed a Bull was sent.
Let loose from Rome, with speed it came,
Daring the King, now known to fame
As Lackland, but more fitting name
I do affirm "John Bull" had been;
Who here, 'mongst English Kings is seen
In carvèd niche in this vast screen,
To whom, of right, three queens belong.
And now a very grievous wrong
I mention to the others done;
For here there's space for only one,

---

* A.D. 1199.

So " place aux dames " we must refuse
To grace the subject of our muse,
Declining to select or choose,
Or to in any way discuss
Charms that are now removed from us.

But concerning clauses sixty and three,
From feudal oppression thy country to free,
Which formed the Great Charter ever to be
The foundation of laws that ye now-a-days see,
A few seconds surely 'tis meet to devote
Awhile on the screen we pause to take note,
And view the meadow of council fair,
With its mighty host in conference there ;
Like the murmuring sound of threatening storm,
The voices combined of that council form.
Then bishop and baron, in conclave assembled,
Their thoughts of aversion but slightly dissembled,
Towards him who ruled the Church and State,
Of which the future weal and fate
Was then suspended in debate.
At length a charter well approved,
By resolution just was moved,
And John constrained to seal and sign,
And thus to sanction their design.
And all the while his soul rebels,
And sullen for a time he dwells
Apart from those 'gainst whom he plans
To plunder them of home and lands.

And foreign aid he needs must ask
To help him in the treacherous task.
Such then the plan by John devised,
And which his barons so surprised,
And, at the moment looked for least,
Changed revel, tournament, and feast
Into a struggle to uphold
The laws at Runnymeade enrolled.
Filled with dismay, their piteous plight
Induced the barons to invite
A neighbour's aid ; as John had done.
And thus was civil war begun.
Then Fortune's tide again was turned,
And retribution was discerned;
For now the tide of ocean sweeps,
And wave on wave exulting leaps
To rob the tyrant of his treasure
Of jewels priceless above measure.
And records none again may trace,
Then scattered were on ocean's face,
All in the " Wash " clean washed away
By force no power on earth can stay.

So heart-sick and weary, that fatal march o'er,
* The King came to Newark, to leave it no more ;
For death soon decreed, he should be there bereft
Of his kingdom and all that the ocean had left.

---

* A.D. 1216.

The latter of right to his firstborn must go;
But England no crown had just then to bestow,
And that symbol of majesty being at sea
'Twas resolved that the brow of the young King should be
Encircled forthwith with a band of gold wire,
Crowns not being easy to borrow or hire.
*And Pembroke who was wise and good
†A sort of sponsor for him stood,
Until, at sixteen years, confirmed
A ruler's duty he had learned.
But all too soon it was he planned
To wrest from France the Norman land,
While this his signal failure must
Have much destroyed his people's trust.
And then it was that civil war,
That foe of order and of law,
Throughout the land again was rife.
In tumult and unseemly strife,
Then brothers were in arms arrayed,
And captive was King Henry made,
Together with the Prince his son,
Whose after valiant conduct won
The right that he should honour claim
And be for ever known to fame
As the first Edward, England's Prince,
Whose namesake and descendant since,

---

* A.D. 1216.   † The Earl of Pembroke was made Protector.

Abroad, at home, alike can claim
All honour to his princely name.

Oh! vain it was to strive to hold
Spirit so daring and so bold;
*And, freedom gained, he next proceeds
To raise an army, which he leads
Against De Montfort, who was slain,
While he who prisoner had been ta'en,
†Their King, in foremost rank they place,
As history says, to their disgrace,
With none as herald to proclaim
The rank of him who thus became
A target for each random blow
That round him laid his subjects low;
While there no royal guard is found
To shield the King on English ground;
And sure his heart within him dies,
As in extremity he cries,
In terror dread his life to save,
Who ne'er had sued, but mercy gave.

And now success has crowned the day.
The crown of England once more may
Assert its power and royal sway.
Of the third Henry what befell
'Tis not my purpose here to tell,

---

* Taken prisoner by Simon de Montfort.   † Henry III.

But of the progress in his reign,
Results of which e'en now ye gain.

And first I name that wise control,
Supplied by England as a whole,
When from both shire and town were chose
Two knights or members, who compose
A council wise, on whom depend
The laws they make or, may be, mend.

*Then first they found the earth could yield
A substance which had lain concealed
Beneath its surface, and which we
With one assent must all agree
Of universal use to be.
Other discoveries followed then,
And foremost of his fellow men
    The Friar Bacon stands,
Worthy of more enlightened age.
What was he but a prophet sage
    Who thus the mind expands?
To grasp at science that would be
A motive power by land and sea;
When that same coal, so lately found
In sable blocks deep in the ground,
Should generate its vapoury haze,
Known now as steam in these our days.

---

* Coal. First charter granted by Henry III. to the town of Newcastle-on-Tyne to dig sea coal A.D. 1239.

And when that true, unerring guide,
Which northward o'er the waters wide
    Points to the distant Pole,
From eastward came, like that pale star
Which shepherds gazed at from afar,
    Awe-struck within the soul,
For full six hundred years the friend
Of mariners, I would contend
For this same compass that it gain,
As first existing in this reign,
    A passing notice here.

Other discoveries, some still used,
And others by mankind abused,
    About this time appear;
By which remark, we comprehend
The poison that distillers vend,
The origin of which we trace
To the wild Moor of tawny race.
And things which now pass unobserved,
First at this time their purpose served,
For Westminster's imposing shrine
Was rebuilt on a fresh design.
And here when fifty years had passed,
King Henry's bones reposed at last,
While he whose turn it next became
To wear the crown, is known to fame
Already by the last Crusade,
Which gained him laurels ne'er to fade.

*"Twas well for Edward he had served
In Palestine, and thus deserved
The confidence that he must gain
Who England's honour would maintain
Against the mountain tribes, who first
From out the west in torrents burst.
But soon, their Prince Llewellyn slain,
Further resistance was in vain ;
And Edward needs but this pretext
That Wales to England be annexed.
And, with the judgment that can weigh
Effect and cause, his plans display
The lawyer skill for which his name
Renowned in Europe then became.

   Son of the soil, their Prince he chose,
   By which diplomacy he shews,
   In that this their native Prince,
   And all who've borne his title since,
   To England's throne the heirs have been
   Destined alike, as will be seen,
   A union to cement between
   The British people of the West
   And those by whom he is confest
   As England's future hope to be,
   From eastern shore to western sea.

---

* A.D. 1272.

Now as from history's earliest date
In rhyme we've chosen to relate
    The changes that have been,
They here a passing comment claim
In whom there dwelt the Poet's flame,
    * The bards of ancient mien,
Who, in the minstrelsy of song,
Pleaded so earnestly and long,
Whether with purpose to awake
For their own home and country's sake,
Zeal in their fellow men;
Or whether theirs the tenderer theme
That ofttimes proves but idle dream,
    Invoking yet again
The Love-god, who, with bended bow,
Can right or left his arrows throw,
Wounding, perchance, where least ye guess,
Because, reluctant to confess,
The victim may disown the power
Which has enthralled life's ev'ry hour.
All this and more, the bards have sung
Awhile their harps wild accents rung.
Welcomed in castle and in cot,
Not without honour was their lot.

Then surely here we must deny,
And boldly dare to give the lie

---

* Druids or Britons.

To that harsh calumny 'gainst Edward's name,
Which history's page has striven to defame;
For just he was, and generous as wise,
Who by a calm, unbiassed judgment tries
The cause of those oppressed who suffer wrong;
In homely phrase, the weak against the strong.
How inconsistent, then, to deem that he
Consent had given to harsh brutality,
For such a statement false, intended by design
The character of Edward with malice to malign,
Is worse than a mere fable, for oft in such we're taught
That in the end a moral may be with meaning fraught;
But to allege that he, the first who did create
The highly-honoured title of Poet Laureate,
Should dire destruction level against the mountain bard!
So monstrous a delusion from these pages we discard.
For as the Modern England began in Edward's reign,
And a legal constitution then followed in its train,
Not only war but peaceful arts made progress under him,
And imaged tales in graceful verse contributed to win
The mind to admiration for the poetry of song,
To which I'd fain description give, but dare not now prolong
The subject that has tempted us from out the beaten track,
From which to history's records we now again turn back.

    To the kingdom of the Northmen,
    Which, albeit, was kingless then,
    'Tis meet that we should now allude,
    Though from such scenes of war and feud

'Tis little knowledge we extract,
Beyond the bare details of fact.
And sure, methinks, if he had known
Who destined was to fill the throne,
That all the honour it would bring
Resulted in the name of King,
Without the freedom that should be
Theirs who enjoy such dignity,
*Baylule had not desired to claim
A title honoured but in name.

For Edward sought a vassal's aid
From the new king his choice had made,
Commanding, as the over-lord,
Homage of person and of sword.
But 'twas in vain, until by force
Of arms he framed a different course,
When Baylule resignation tendered,
In other words, his throne surrendered;
And Edward, temperate and just,
Decides Earl Surrey to entrust
With power to govern and extend
A pardon free, while to defend
The English rights, his aim and end;
Until again rebellion rose,
And discontent the power o'erthrows
That peace and order have restored,
While vested in the over-lord,

---

* Baliol—Balliol, originally Baylule.

And by an outlaw, as 'tis said,
The Lowland army then was led,
Offers of peace by whom rejected,
We'd style them now the disaffected;
Whose leader proved himself to be
A champion for their liberty.
For such was William Wallace, Knight,
Who dared to question feudal right,
When yeoman and peasant to arms he calls,
Besieging old Stirling's castle walls,
Who with consummate skill contrived to defeat
Earl Surrey and left him in full retreat,
When northward the banner of Edward came
With the host, who enlist in the royal name.
And the King in person, with fixed intent
The insult to Surrey forthwith to resent,
At Falkirk a signal victory gains,
Whereby the rule he still maintains,
Although unconquered the country remains,
That Wallace had roused with a patriot's zeal
Her true position to see and to feel.
And though Edward had formed the wise design,
The North with the South as one to combine,
By a general amnesty, to all who shared
In the late revolt, with those who dared
To question his right and lawful will,
And who yet the governing power held still,
All but he who had refused
And Edward's clemency abused,

Of treason, sacrilege accused,
And who his crimes to expiate
At Smithfield met a penal fate.

Now in this sketch we've striven to shew,
Whether it be to friend or foe,
That in the motto of his youth
The King upheld the law of truth
And all admonished to keep troth,
For sacred every liegeman's oath,
Whether in fealty to the throne,
Or sworn to one, and one alone;
And that King Edward loved his Queen,
Whose children numbered all fifteen,
And long his consort who had been,
Proof have we yet, as may be seen,
In those memorials of her worth,
Where, on its way to mother earth,
The body rested on the track
From which no body ere turns back.
So on each spot he placed a cross
To shew how much he mourned her loss.
But no memorial, I'll engage,
The monarch's sorrow could assuage
Until he was, as we are told,
Again by marriage rite consoled.

But of domestic peace how few
His days—though into years he grew,
When towards the North again he drew

To war with Bruce, who rose to claim
The Scottish crown and kingly name,
And who by murderous deed commenced
The raids, which Edward so incensed
Against an enemy whose power
Not shelter sought from fort or tower,
But from defences nature gave,
Sequestered glen and mountain cave.
But vain the vow that Edward made,
Although he summoned to his aid
A mighty army, as 'tis said,
For death demands a flag of truce
Ere he could battle give to Bruce;
While to his son he then bequeathed
The contest ere his last he breathed—
A legacy that suited ill
The taste, or habits, or the will
Of one who destined was to fill
The throne of him whose sun was set—
First Edward of Plantagenet.

In the hey-day of youth how the heart bounds free,
Like the gallant bark rides o'er a following sea!
Then steady, my lads! watch well how ye steer
On the ocean of life, and see your course clear,
For the rocks and the quicksands that lie on the way
May soon into danger thy manhood betray;
Nor companion with those who, by word and by deed,
In the pathway of error would craftily lead,

Till both judgment and reason are overboard cast,
And shipwrecked the life that is falsely called fast;

>*A moral which, to illustrate
>By young Carnarvon's luckless fate,
>Return we to th' historic page
>Which chronicles that early age,
>And see the father's counsel wise
>His youthful, headstrong son despise.
>Who haughty Gaveston recalls,
>And by his fatal influence falls,
>Nor made one effort to fulfil
>The anxious wish of him, whose will
>To England as the law had been
>For years, as we've already seen.
>
>So leaving Scotland to its fate,
>And all his followers in a strait,
>Young Edward seeks a foreign mate;
>Who, like her country, named "La Belle,"
>He loved not wisely but too well.
>And so resolved not long to wait
>For his fair bride. The marriage date
>And coronation both appear
>To have occurred in the same year.

But foes were made of those who had been friends,
And vainly 'gainst the barons he contends;

---

* A.D. 1307.

Who, in defiance of their Sovereign's will,
Removed the hand of Gaveston on Blacklow Hill;
A personal offence which no man can resent
But which to Edward proved a plea for discontent.
Which was by no means mended, as our tragic sequel shews,
When in Hugh de Spenser and his son fresh favourites he chose,
Who both were hanged and quartered by these above-named foes.

> Then famine, with her face of abject woe,
> For full three years attacked both high and low,
> Whose ravages the people so depressed,
> That to obey his father's last behest,
> By him neglected some six years ago,
> Resulted now in Edward's overthrow;
> Who too late was aroused to redeem the time lost,
> As hereafter he bitterly found to his cost.

Weak and irresolute, with no concern
The tactics of leader or general to learn,
What marvel Edward failed at Bannockburn!
And where so many nations brave appeared in arms allied,
Who never had before been called to combat side by side,
For wild marauders fresh from Wales, likewise from Erin's Isle,
With Neustria and Gascony supplied the rank and file;
But as where discipline is not, disorder sure is rife,
It ended in a deadly and most disastrous strife;
And Scotland's freedom was complete
By reason of this same defeat.

Alas! for thee, O luckless King,
Scarce had a score of years ta'en wing,
Ere thou, unfit to rule declared
By one consent, which nobles shared,
Thy crown art called on to resign,
A sentence stern but most condign,
And further comment we decline.

Then from Edward of Carnarvon we now may take our leave;
Meanwhile his heir and eldest son prepare we to receive;
*This time an English fortress a birth-place and a name
†Gives to the youthful monarch who comes the crown to claim,
Who ere a score of summers had well passed o'er his head
Was destined England's throne to fill, a Dutch princess to wed,
Who to her kingly husband, and to his kingdom's cause
Her love and duty proved by aiding in the wars
Resumed by King Edward, his right to repeat
To the crown of the Scotch, who then suffered defeat
At Halidon Hill, with a serious loss,
And again at the battle of Neville's Cross,
When Philippa, a heroine brave,
To Scotland's King free lodgings gave,
And whom to England then they took,
While John of France was brought to book

---

* Edward III., surnamed Windsor.   † A.D. 1327.

* For aiding David, though in vain,
In his endeavour to retain
The crown and kingdom which was lost.
Nor counted John, it seems, the cost
Of thus defending Scotland's throne;
By doing which he lost his own,
And shared his brother monarch's fate,
Alike a prisoner of the State.

While victory the English crowned,
Who then became likewise renowned
    At Cressy and Poictiers,
The arms of England's sable Prince,
Whose fame has been recorded since,
    Through some five hundred years;
A kingdom's conqueror was he,
But destined ne'er a king to be;
For though well-earned, in valiant fight,
The golden spurs he gained as knight,
Yet came not from without the foe
That laid the heir of England low.
For human strength once undermined
Not long will soul and body bind.
Then from the son we turn again
Awhile to the third Edward's reign,
Inventions and events to scan
Which at this period began
Their influence to exert on man.

---

    * David, second King of Scotland.

And first we learn, the city gate
Enclosed within the civic state,
Where loyal subjects of the crown
Assumed the aldermanic gown
And he they chose to fill the chair
Received the title of Lord Mayor.

Then next, it seems, the House of Peers
And Commons were set by the ears,
And so the House, it was decided
Once and for all must be divided.
And the Commons no longer sit cheek by jowl
With the coronet and the priestly cowl.
The latter profess to be men of peace
Who pray that all wars and tumults may cease,
* Then 'tis passing strange that a monk should be,
The importer of arms and artillerie;
† While he of St Albans was more saintlike
For 'twas only a clock that he made to strike,
To put you up to the time of day
When perchance you are passing Westminster way,
Or should you ever at midnight stray
To contemplate the Abbey grey,
Outlined beneath the moon's pale ray.
But hold! Ill-luck to him who tries
Th' inconstant moon to eulogise,
And time forbids with warning finger
That here too long we may not linger;

---

* Schwartz. † Abbot of St. Albans, 1368.

And for this reason 'tis that we
Omit in this our historie,
Each person and event to note
Which otherwise 'twere right to quote.

*Then next 'tis Richard, a boy King,
Whom here we to your notice bring,
To whom the surname was ascribed
Which from his birthplace he derived;
The same, a western port of France,
The trade in wine has seen advance,
Till taste and title of Bordeaux
Are in the mouths of high and low.

'Tis of the second Richard, then,
Who, as the King of Englishmen,
Was early called upon to fill
A throne where firm resolve and will
Were greatly needed to repress
From those oft ready to redress
Their fancied wrongs, and who were led
To take offence, because the head,
The thinking portion, or the brain,
The subject of a tax became.
But bravely then, as history tells,
The tumult raised young Richard quells.
Who next was called on to oppose
Invasion made by foreign foes;

* A.D. 1377.

To wit, the French, who entered Forth
To join the army from the North,
When Perth, Dunedin, and Dundee,
With some beside th'aforesaid three,
Suffered for their temerity.
And in Northumbria, we learn,
Was fought the fight of Otterburn,
Wherefrom the origin we trace
Of the old rhyme called "Chevy Chase."

And here a tribute to the lines,
Writ by the men of early times
   'Tis meet that we devote ;
When Chaucer, Poet Laureate,
Renowned in this his day and date,
   Of Canterbury wrote
The tales that gained him endless fame
And left him an undying name.
But when from out the Tabard Inn,
Where doubtless all was snug within,
Say, was it to atone for sin,
That they a pilgrimage begin
To the old prelate's lonely shrine,
As if some mystic charm divine
Existed in a few dry bones,
Encased beneath the Abbey stones ?

And now farewell to thee, Bordeaux,
Alike a slave to pomp and show,

In whom we mark the sad decline
Of the Plantagenets' name and line,
In the year of grace thirteen nine nine.

So then the House they call "Red Rose"
To power supreme in England grows,
And Lancaster usurps the crown
Which Richard then compelled lays down :
And by a bold determined stroke
Proclaimed as king was Bolingbroke.
By valour was the victory won
With which the Red Rose power begun ;
By valour was that power maintained
Which erst by valour had been gained.
Witness the fight of Hateley field
Where the bold Percy's doom was sealed,
Who, but a few short months before
Proudly a victor's honour bore.
At Homildon Hill where, as it is said,
Earl Douglas and others an army had led,
And who as prisoners there were ta'en,
By him who was at Hateley slain.
Events long past, but unforgot,
For peace there dwells, and strife is not
In that small church which marks the spot ;
But he who there the structure placed,
And of whose reign events we've traced,
Too little knew of that same peace,
While troubles with his years increase,

And without trial or good reason,
*A bishop, who was charged with treason,
Then lost his head; not that I mean
His wits departed, as 'twould seem,
But that the casket which contains
The mental gifts men call their brains,
Was by a piece of great ill-luck
At one stroke from his body struck.

And Sawtree too, St. Osyth's priest,
Like ox prepared for Christmas feast,
Exposed to influence of fire
A living man there to expire,
†First of that noble brotherhood,
The martyrs, for their faith who've stood
Unflinchingly 'midst terrors nigh,
For do they not e'en then descry
The home where spirits never die?

To sanction such foul deeds, I wot,
On Henry's memory left a blot,
O'er which we fain would draw a veil,
And pass on to the next entail;
‡ Young Henry Fifth at Monmouth born,
And who was suited to adorn
Alike the council and the field
By traits of character revealed

---

*Scrope, Archbishop of York.   † A.D. 1401.   ‡ A.D. 1413.

During a short but splendid reign,
Where he contrived in France to gain
A power which manifest was made
When he that kingdom dared invade.
Then Harfleur, and then Agincourt,
Were with success and prudence fought
* 'Gainst those who deemed his tactics sport,
And who could scarely have believed
Their judgment had been so deceived.
But power acquired by England's throne
Extended not in France alone,
For England in this reign began
† Her naval armament to man,
Which destined was to rule the sea
And pride of Englishmen to be ;

While customs then considered new
Without a doubt most useful grew
As many a soul in London knew;
And so it chanced that by an Act
Of Parliament, by Henry backed,
‡ Each house was made to shew a light ;
So then a jovial luckless wight
Returning to his home at night,
Found by the door, him to await,
A candle placed to guide his gait.

---

* Tennis balls were sent by the Dauphin of France in derision.
† Henry V. was the first monarch who established a permanent navy.
‡ A.D. 1485.

Then bless the days when no latch keys
Invented were to plague and teaze,
When none had heard of Mr. Chubb,
Whose name now often gets a rub,
When every means the holder tries
His skill and forethought can devise
To fix the key which he applies
Into his castle's outer oak,
Till by one bold and dext'rous stroke,
And which in France a "coup" they call,
He finds himself within his hall,
Then pauses not, but seeks his mate,
At once resolved to meet his fate,
And see if she has grown irate
'Gainst him for staying out so late.
Perchance he finds her well-content ;
Perchance the interval she spent
By following inclination's bent;
And as her lord has done the same,
It rather seems she's not to blame !
Then with a moral somewhat stale
Complete we our digressive tale.
'Tis this, that 'twould be well to choose
Diversions which would both amuse,
Nor oft indulge in so-called larks,
With which we close these sage remarks.

That brevity's the soul of wit
I take is a decided hit,

And due regard, in these our rhymes,
To Harry Monmouth's reign and times
Already has to him been paid,
Who from these records now must fade,
And to his only son give place,
The last of the Lancastrian race,
And who derives his second name,
As the third Edward did the same,
From Windsor, of historic fame;
Whose life, ere counted 'twas by years,
A life of trouble soon appears,
And who, an infant monarch crowned,
Stern fortune on his childhood frowned.

Needs must we, then, the scene now change,
Where by coincidence most strange
* Two kings in one year, as it seems,
Were, one in Paris, one at Rheims,
Both crowned, while one their end and aim,
Supreme o'er France to rule and reign,
Which Henry claimed as right bequeathed
Ere the late King his last had breathed.
Not so with Charles, who now uprose
Both claim and treaty to oppose,
Who not in his own strength relied,
Nor in the men who by his side
For him would loyally have died;

---

* A.D. 1430.

But in a humble peasant maid,
With sword in hand, in mail arrayed,
Whom Heaven in its wisdom chose
To save her country from its foes,
And whose command she straight obeys
*The siege of Orleans to raise,
Fulfilling her ambitious dreams
When Charles in triumph enters Rheims.

There was he crowned in royal state,
While history's records then relate
The maiden at his side did wait,
And over him the sword still bore
Which had good service done before.
Was ever there a guard so fair,
Or one who more could do or dare
For sake of King and country's laws,
Of whom she had espoused the cause?
But her commission now fulfilled,
Home to return the maiden willed,
†To Voges valley, whence she came,
Not seeking for reward or fame.
And oh! how fatal the delay
By which she was induced to stay!
What mattered it to her or hers
The noble titles Charles confers,
Who is of France the acknowledged lord,
By virtue of that maiden's sword,

---

* A.D. 1430.   † On the old frontiers of Lorraine.

While she a prisoner has been ta'en
By the Burgundians at Compeigne?
And who are they that instigate
The process of her tragic fate?

Is it the men of iron nerve
Who, trained to arms, their country serve?
Not so! from out the Church's pale
Deeds that would make the boldest quail
Enacted were, so runs my tale,
By Cochou, Bishop of Beauvais;
A fact no author can gainsay.
And none the tide of fury stemmed,
'Gainst one whom Mother Church condemned
To torture and a cruel death,
But who, ere yielding up her breath,
Upheld a faith which naught could shake,
When hurried to the burning stake.
Divines miscalled were those I trow,
Who summoned from the powers below
That fiery element of woe.
But fiends who from their brethren borrow
A scourge of agony and sorrow,
To punish one all innocent
Of malice, or of wrong intent.

But shun we now the scene of pain
Where after sympathy is vain;
Nor would I wish at length to dwell
On all the sorrows which befell

The English King, whose luckless fate
Perforce we briefly must relate.
Of kingdom and of throne deprived,
For ten long years he yet survived,
To see one of the White Rose race
Supplant the Red Rose in its place,
A wound no earthly power had healed,
Till death at length the record sealed.

*And whence this youth from o'er the sea,
Who King of England claims to be,
In Rouen's ancient city born,
With manners, courage to adorn
The sovereignty he dares to take
As heir of his long-dead namesake?
From the third Edward he descends,
Who as fourth Edward now ascends
The throne, which during half his reign
His enemies dispute in vain.
A widow then he made a wife,
Whereby fresh discontent and strife
Engendered were, by Warwick led,
Because the bride the King had wed,
And she who in his eyes finds grace
Can nothing boast of royal race.

Maker of kings, the title Warwick earned,
A strange one truly; but if he had learned

---

* A.D. 1461.

Likewise to honour her who had a subject been,
Good will he'd gained from him who made her queen.
But 'twas not so, for thousands fought and bled
Ere yet the White Rose triumphed o'er the Red;
Then Warwick and his cause together fell
On Barnet's field, as old historians tell,
And Edward reigns in pomp of youthful pride.
His charms of person were by none denied,
And fatal proved to one, if not to more,
Referring to the luckless Mistress Shore,
Whose husband plied his craft in Lombard Street,
As in a worthy citizen was meet;
Perchance then dreaming that the hours of toil
Were well repaid when Jane should reap the spoil,
But who ere long her home and lord forsakes,
And to th' unwelcome truth the good man then awakes,
Concerning whom the records naught unfold;
But soon or late no doubt he was consoled,
As mankind when they're wronged, not in the wrong,
When reason comes to aid, grieve seldom long;
While she, who for the wrong deserves the blame,
Has handed down a most unworthy name;
But Shoreditch even now, I will contend,
Is a cognomen 'twould be well to mend.
What matters it that one the title bore—
A baron, so 'tis said—in olden days of yore?
The name is always coupled with that of Mistress Shore.

    And now I must awhile detain
    The reader, briefly to explain

Why Earl of March was title fit
For him who on the throne did sit:
Because the March of intellect,
On which men now so oft reflect,
Received its greatest help and aid
* By the invention Caxton made,
The most important ever known,
Into perfection which has grown
In this the day ye call your own;
For mind with mind may hold converse,
And knowledge far and wide disperse,
While e'en our muse, expressed in verse,
Had fallen dead, we must confess,
Without Will Caxton's printing press.
Honour to this man good and true
Should, then, from all the world be due!

And now the reign of the first White Rose
In this brief review must draw to a close.
As the Earl of March quietly turns up his toes,
† And leaves to his son of tender age
The throne as a goodly heritage,
Who though he kingly title bore
Yet crown of England never wore.
And though historians still debate
The subject of young Edward's fate,
Who deem untimely death his doom,
Because for his uncle he made room,

---

* A.D. 1473.   † A.D. 1483.

And present at whose coronation,
He thus accepts the situation,
In gorgeous garb and brave array,
For which the nation had to pay,
As there in crimson cloth of gold,
With velvet lined each ample fold,
And royal purple robe likewise,
But somewhat shorter made in size,
Which lined with richest damask green
Was for a lad not yet fourteen
I take it rather out of place,
Although he came of kingly race ;
While stomacher and doublet made
Of satin, his slim form displayed,
And velvet bonnet over all
Completes a garb we now should call
Best suited for a fancy ball.

And furthermore 'tis passing strange
To mark the latitude or range,
Which those indulge who would disguise
The truth amid a pack of lies,
And who a tragedy invent,
With mischievous and wrong intent,
King Richard's conduct to malign
* To serve the heir of Tudor's line,

---

* Improbable and notorious falsehood. Walpole's Historic Doubts, page 51.

And who against an English King
The charge of murder dare to bring,
Sully the annals of the land
When Richard's name they foully brand;
And as the guilty most times dread
Where danger leads the path to tread,
'Tis marvel that this King should fight
At Bosworth for his crown and right,
And fought he bravely none deny
Who doomed was on that field to die.

And next we see how it befell
That love e'en civil war can quell,
For Red and White Rose both unite,
When man and maid their troth do plight;
As he who won on Bosworth field,
The Tudor, thus the compact sealed,*
When for his bride and queen he chose
The daughter of the first White Rose.

And if a crafty policy can make a monarch great,
Well formed King Henry was to rule in matters of the State,
Who treasure heaped, of vast amount,
By millions as we now might count;
And who his revenues to draw,
Extorted them by force of law,
And by his contracts with the Jews,
To deal in gold who ne'er refuse.

---

* A.D. 1485.   † Elizabeth, daughter of Edward IV.

But 'tis to the wall of the silver sea,
That the country owes her security,
And deeming that commerce 'twere wise to preserve,
And to rule o'er the ocean that purpose would serve,
He sends his great namesake a vessel of war
By the might of her strength to protect British law;
And as a new world had been born in this reign *
And the credit was claimed by the nation of Spain,
So likewise resolved a new land to found
The King employed Cabot the ocean to sound;
And when with success was his enterprise crowned,
They called it Newfoundland, that land which they found.
As they sailed to the West, so they sailed to the East,
In importance the last, was by no means the least,
As one Vasco de Gama discovered the scope
Of the world, as he rounded the Cape of Good Hope,
Was greater than ever he dreamed of before,
Which good hope already him led to explore,
And that Neptune a passage to India allowed
Through those his dominions not hitherto ploughed.

All these and some other events in the reign
Of this, the first Tudor, to dwell on were vain.
Suffice it to say, that the King has enshrined
His memory and bones in a building, designed
By himself it may be, for we know he erected
The chapel which now with his name is connected;

---

* A.D. 1498.

And where, with the richest of tracery lined
The skill of the architect so has designed
That the style of the walls and the roof be combined
To shew an example, the purest and best,
Of the Gothic so-called, as it must be confessed,
And that such has the progress of ages defied,
Although like the river that runs by its side,
Time onward pursueth its swift flowing tide.

    While here in silent beds of stone
    Sleep generations past and gone,
    Imaged in marble or in brass,
    Gazed on by idlers as they pass,
    Say, where is now their pride of power?
    Gone like the sunshine of an hour!
    Say, where is now their pomp of State?
    Gone, by a like decree of fate,
    Are they within the narrow bed
    Where rest beneath the so-called dead?
    A thousand times I say thee nay!
    Mind dwelleth not in mouldering clay.

    For it is a germ of the life divine
    That dwelleth alway with thee and thine,
    And alone resisteth the flight of time;
    Unseen 'twas ever, though known to be here,
    Unseen it is still though ever 'tis near;
    And the tenant departing changes not,
    Though the dwelling deserted decay and rot.

Then up and be doing, and leave behind
A name regarded by all mankind,
And deathless shall be the sound of thy name,
For in thy works thou shalt live again!

But here let us pause and a moment take breath,
As we turn from the portal and presence of death,
To gaze on a monarch, the next of his line,
Who commenced rule in England in 1509;
His father a throne has left him by right,
A legacy which had been gained in fair fight,
And Arthur, his brother, that throne's previous heir,
Has left also a wife, we are told passing fair;
But the latter we scarce can a legacy call,
For no will save their own was consulted at all.

Now concerning the sister of a deceased wife,
Which at present in England is causing some strife,
I suppose that the same, when a man's brother dies,
Concerning the widow is binding likewise.
But I cannot say whether such law then existed,
Or if, in the face of it, Henry persisted
In wooing the lady, without dispensation
From prelate or priest, or the world's approbation.
But this much I know, that the Queen was betrayed
In believing that lasting the contract was made.
But eighteen years passed, when his purpose to suit,
King Henry his marriage resolved to refute,

Which declared he invalid because he had wed
The Lady Anne Boleyn already instead.

While Catherine's sad and lonely fate
Was matter made for sage debate
'Twixt Henry and the Holy See,
On which point neither could agree.
Allegiance then the King denies,
All Papal thunders he defies,
And to the Parliament applies
To make him head as it would seem,
And ruler of the Church supreme ;
A point which, in its culmination,
Resulted in the Reformation.
A scandal grave he then removed,
And by his power despotic proved
Against the Church of Rome too true,
And which from her corruption grew ;
But good from evil ofttimes leads,
As from the monks and their misdeeds,
At length the Church of England springs,
And changes all the face of things.

Catherine meanwhile neglected dies,
But Anne not long her place supplies,
And soon has cause to rue the day
That first she stood in Catherine's way ;
For it became her luckless fate
To find, alas ! when all too late,

Her husband's love had turned to hate.
She was condemned to lose her head,
And on the morrow thrice was wed
The fickle King, of whose next wife
We little know, but that her life
Was short, and that her maiden name
Was Seymour, with the prefix Jane ;
But in this case 'twas nature did
The work whereby the King was rid
Of her ere many months had passed,
Though Jane by no means was the last
With him who shared the English throne ;
For Henry, once more left alone,
Sent, as we're given to understand,
The offer of his royal hand
By emissaries to suggest,
In any manner they judged best,
A lady suited to his views ;
And now mark well what next ensues !
To him a portrait then they brought,
By which, it seems, bluff Hal was caught ;
And well the artist him deceives
In representing Anne of Cleves,
As fashioned fair in beauty's mould !
But lo ! the sequel needs be told ;
As of offence against the laws
That fatal portrait was the cause ;
For soon the King expressed his will
That this his marriage should be *nil*,

*"And what is worse, he lost his head
Who first advised the King to wed
This German Princess, who became
A wife divorced, but free from blame.

And ere six months had passed away,
Since the last royal marriage day,
With little time for wise debate,
The King proceeds to celebrate
His nuptials with another mate,
The niece of Norfolk, Howard called,
A second Catherine Queen, installed,
And who the penalty soon paid,
For Henry accusation made
Seeking her past life to retrace,
As history says to her disgrace.
But 'tis no part of ours to pry
Into the wherefore and the why
Of Catherine Howard's cruel fate,
Which only we commiserate.
Four spinsters thus, as we have seen,
To Henry had in turn been Queen.
Then where is she will take their place
Or dare the situation face;
Where dangers and domestic strife
Not only peril peace, but life?
She only who has once been wife,

---

* Thomas Cromwell, July 28th, 1540.

A prudent widow, proves her skill,
Where others failed the post to fill ;
And Lady Catherine Parr survives
The monarch who had owned six wives,
Whose reign commenced with promise bright
And at Teronne he gained the fight *
Whereat his foes, like coward curs,
Plied most the weapons known as spurs ;

While like success his arms attends,
At Flodden Field, when he contends
'Gainst James the Fourth, who there was slain,
For which he'd but himself to blame.
For meddling with dispute is wrong
When such to others doth belong ;
And surely this, one would have thought,
A warning lesson might have taught
To James the Fifth, but 'twas not so,
Who some years later needs must go
England to fight, on her own ground
At Solway, where defeat he found ;
And sheltered him in dire despair
Within the walls of Falkland, where
Came soon the end of all his grief,
As silent death brought him relief.

But for a while now let us cease
These tales of war and speak of peace,

---

* In France, and known as the Battle of Spurs.

Where Henry and the King of France
Were met to view the tilt and ancle,
Broke but in fair and friendly fight
'Twixt lordly baron and true knight.
In truth it was a glorious sight!
That field outspread, as we are told,
Resembled most a "cloth of gold."

And if with pageants such as these
King Henry strove himself to please,
What wonder his resources went,
His fortune all too soon was spent,
And to obtain him fresh supplies
To trusted Wolsey he applies—
A generous man, sincere and kind,
Who to his sovereign, then we find,
His town and country house assigned,
Whitehall and Hampton Court to wit,
Both which he then proceeds to quit
As proof of his devotion true,
Which none than Henry better knew;
But with ingratitude most base
Must needs the Cardinal displace,
And who, they say, of grief soon died,
Or of, it may be, wounded pride.

Now of a sovereign six times wed
Much more there doubtless might be said.
A handsome person and a cultured mind
Were both in him in early youth combined;

But selfishness ruled in his inmost soul,
And avarice prompted to like control,
Until at length his legs, the cause of ill,
Carried him off at last, against his will;
And from his London Palace of Whitehall
He takes a farewell leave for good and all.

Three days and nights the secret well was kept,
That of her King the country was bereft,
Though to his son the throne had been bequeathed,
Not long before his last the late King breathed,
*And of young Edward, who, although a youth,
A knowledge shews beyond his years; in truth,
So few the years that he o'er England reigned,
'Tis wonder where the wisdom had been gained,
Which founded schools at such an early age,
Evincing thus a forethought deep and sage.

In modern verse we find that love and war,
Though strange companions, often coupled are,
But here we have an instance where they twain
Acknowledged as effect and cause became;
When Somerset's endeavour to fulfil
Instructions given in the late King's will,
Touching the marriage of the Prince, his son,
Led to the fight, in which the English won,
At Musselburgh, where they advanced to face
The Scottish army, left in evil case;

---

* A.D. 1547.

A boy of half a score of summers then,
Counselled by some sixteen appointed men.
Such was the young King Edward, sixth, and last
Who of his name appear in history past.

And of his generation and his day,
Some few facts here take note of by the way,
When Leeds and Wakefield (known as clothing towns)
'Gan to be valued on commercial grounds;
And first were coined both sixpences and crowns.
Now Lord Lieutenants were originated,
And priests were first permitted to be mated.
But to return to Edward, whose young day
Scarce yet had dawned ere it had ebbed away,
*And Lady Grey they then proclaim,
Who Queen of England then became,
For Edward's will it was, and not her own,
Which caused her to accept the proffered throne.
Oh, sad her fate the female first that reigned,
Who but for thirteen days the rule retained,
Then seized, deposed, and with her husband slain.
Such was the tragic fate of Lady Jane.

† The late King's sister now the throne ascends,
'Gainst whom in vain Northumberland contends,
For she his army to her standard won,
Ere yet her rule could scarce be called begun.

---

* A.D. 1553.   † A.D. 1553.

*Then marries Philip, who a king became
In his own right, and soon returned to Spain,
Leaving the Queen, whose love was unrequited,
To mourn the prospect of the life he'd blighted.
Soured by suspicion, and by nature proud,
Freedom of conscience Mary disallowed.
Bigot she was and by her mandate cruel
Bishops and laymen were made human fuel,
The fires of persecution then to feed,
Only because they differed from her creed,
And with the Church of Rome had disagreed;
Whose doctrines though Queen Mary now restores
Not long supreme were held on English shores,
But like a flickering taper soon went dead
And England's Church, whate'er dissensions spread
Never shall own the Pope of Rome
Again to be the head.

But 'tis not mine the province here
To dwell on scenes of rage and fear,
Enough the bloodshed, and the blows,
Dealt by the hand of foreign foes,
While to a fishing-town and port
Of France we next direct a thought,
Which years long since was dearly bought,
When the third Edward claimed his right
To Calais in victorious fight,

---

* Philip, son of Charles V. of Germany, and afterwards King of Spain.

Which took two centuries and more
Ere Frenchmen could their rule restore;
But in the year fifteen five eight,
When Mary's death likewise we date,
Was Calais, after eight days' siege,
Retaken by the Duke of Guise,
For loss of which the Queen so grieved
That she in very truth believed
Her throbbing heart, in death when chill,
Would bear the name of Calais still
Engraved in letters plain to see,
Which was but mental phantasy.

*Now approach we the days of the good Queen Bess,
With a deference, we must needs confess,
In speaking of one who alone then stood
In the pride of her youth and her maidenhood,
And who vigour of mind had long acquired
By habits of study in hours retired,
And whose judgment sound has been oft admired
By her subjects' proud posterity.
She reigned both long and gloriously,
And raised her country the rank to claim,
From henceforth linked with the English name,
To a first-rate power, which it then became;
And such for ever it will remain
While there is a fleet on the ocean wave
Manned by the men who are steady and *brave*

As those who served under Lord Howard and Drake,
With Raleigh and others, commissioned to take
The ships fitted out by King Philip of Spain
In revenge, or in pique, for a suit which was vain ;
And small blame to Queen Bess, who decides to refuse
The proposal to stand in her dead sister's shoes.
Who mounted, with breastplate, and bâton in hand,
Soon lets the troops know who takes the command.
But at length the Armada appears within sight,
And our seamen, desirous to give them fair fight,
From Plymouth to Calais the offer renewed,
And on the west coast was a like chase pursued ;
While the elements also took part in the fray,
And a storm aided greatly the general dismay,
'Till the English at length had it all their own way.
And of that great Armada, "invincible" termed,
But a few shattered cripples to Spain ere returned,
While the power of Old England o'er ocean extends,
And in every direction her vessels she sends ;
Not alone as an island her rights to maintain,
For she's queen of the sea, and enthroned on the main.
But to seek for the lands hitherto all unknown,
Which when found the discoverer may claim as his own ;
And thus her dominion abroad to secure
Which, through future ages, long, long shall endure.

While at home the religion established by law
Being Protestant made, the Pope declares war,
With all his anathemas 'gainst the good Queen,
But little she cared for his thunders, I ween,

Though the laws 'gainst the Romanists, as it seems clear,
In retaliation were made more severe.
And now we must briefly allude to the fate
Of the lovely Queen Mary, though sad to relate,
Who by some ill-advice had dared to presume
Elizabeth's title and rights to assume,
While the title of Queen of the Scots she retained
Was merely a semblance when James, her son, reigned,
And Mary a captive in England became,
Without kingdom or throne, a queen but in name,
Who eighteen long years in captivity spends,
Till a violent death that captivity ends.

But once more to return to the bonny Queen Bess,
Who loved dancing, and mirth, and the splendour of dress,
Who footed it gaily, with toe and with heel,
And it must be confessed, with commendable zeal,
When in years well advanced
Still Her Majesty danced,
And flirted, coquetted, in manner as gay
As she did in the zenith of youth's proud day.
While thus of life's pleasures enjoying a share,
The good of her people was likewise her care;
So literature flourished as seen in this reign,
And the architects likewise have borrowed her name,
Which some call the Tudor, all one and the same;
And the poets and dramatists during that age,
Among them one numbered whose oft quoted page
Replete is with its maxims, both varied and sage,
And claims for him honour as Prince of the Stage;

Whose writings, translated, are well known to most
Of the nations of Europe, who make it a boast
That their knowledge of Shakespeare is fully as good
As if they his original tongue understood.

Advancement, quick as flight of time,
The object is of our design,
And therefore it becomes our task
Apology to crave or ask
From all those gentlemen of note,
Whose names we may neglect to quote,
For authors, poets, learnèd men,
Became somewhat abundant then,
And Spenser of another queen,
Whose like on earth was never seen,
Discourses and so well describes
That centuries his verse survives.

But not in literature alone
The progress of the age is shewn,
Nor in the architectural skill,
Which edifices raised at will,
Like that we see hard by Cornhill,
The Royal Exchange, which first uprose
On the same site where still it shews
An evidence of that advance
At which we here can only glance;
Likewise remarking by the way
That things in use now every day,

Imported then at first became,
Which also we but briefly name.

As from the West potatoes, and from the East came tea,
And Tobago sent tobacco, across the Atlantic sea.
All these and more are but a few
Of manifold discoveries new,
    Which happened in this reign,
As from Elizabeth's accession
England dates her wide progression,
    Continuing such to gain.
And Westminster's right merry peal *
No other past events reveal,
But that which one November day,
The seventeenth, historians say,
    A queen to England gave ;
Who lasting benefits conferred
By every act and deed and word,
    And for the right was brave.
Order maintaining in her court,
The Maiden Queen held that to sport
With woman, unless her consent
Had been to the proceedings lent,
Was 'gainst the law a flagrant wrong
Which guards the weak against the strong.
But little boots it here to dwell
On what in olden times befell

---

* Westminster Abbey bells still ring on the anniversary of Queen Elizabeth's accession.

All those who dared the rules transgress,
Enacted then by good Queen Bess.
For centuries three since then have passed,
But still unchanged her code shall last,
And he who dares a kiss to steal
The theft e'en now must needs conceal;
And she who most herself respects
Is the best champion of her sex,
Resenting all behaviour rude
But not by any means a prude.
So when Lord Essex dared to turn
His back, his ear was made to burn,
Who round did on his axis slew,
As planets are supposed to do,
Then quickly to the sword he wore
He clapped his hand, and may be swore.
Poor man! He could do nothing more.

 But time here fails, that we should dwell
On what hereafter him befell,
For 'tis with sovereigns we've to do
And tributary names but few,
Though as the Queen took so to heart
His death, that 'tis surmised in part
Her own was hastened by regret
For one her love could not forget;
And therefore Essex' name has been
Brought forward in the closing scene
Of this time-honoured, ancient Queen.

*And side by side Elizabeth by her sister Queen was laid,
Beneath a ponderous monument by time yet undecayed,
Who in their creed were bitterest foes,
But now one grave doth both enclose,
And in the holy burial place
Which the first Tudor's bones encase
Here lies the last of Tudor's race.

And next the House of Stuart comes,
Whose four not over-brilliant sons
    Each in review must stand.
† The eldest born of whom was James,
The first who two-fold title claims
    As King of British land.
Shrewd and sagacious was he, but so vain
That e'en these qualities did him but gain
The ridicule of those o'er whom he ruled,
And who by pedantry would not be fooled.
And of King James perhaps 'tis well to say—
The less the better is the better way;
For drunkenness, while not of crimes the least,
Incites to deeds that make man worse than beast.

What wonder, then, if the first Stuart's reign
By gross conspiracies soon marked became?
For discontentment treachery begot,
Which culminated in Gunpowder Plot.

---

* A.D. 1603.   † A.D. 1603.

Erewhile events long afterwards disclose
How King and Parliament were mutual foes.
'Twas then that James, his royal purse to swell,
The rank of peer and baronet did sell;
And towns in Holland would not longer hold,
Which likewise bartered he through greed of gold;
And 'twas for money also Raleigh bought
His liberty, soon after set at naught.

Buildings of brick were now in London seen,
Where only those of wood before had been,
And pipes for water next designed were laid,
Which element became the means of trade
To companies, who from it profit made.
Then to divines, in number forty-eight,
Was Holy Scripture trusted to translate.
What various versions gave they to the task
It boots but little now for us to ask;
Suffice it, that the version authorised
Was in the space of some three years devised,
And not long afterwards the Pilgrim band
*One Christmas morn on Plymouth rock did land,
Who in the "May Flower" had from England sailed,
And now another England New first hailed.

For two-and-twenty years as monarch reigns
The Sixth of Scotland, First of England James,
From whom the nation little profit gains.

---

* A.D. 1620.

Then let us pass from this our brief review
To yet another, strange as it is true,
*Concerning Charles, the late King's son and heir,
Who next assumes the rule of England fair.
But ere he had succeeded to the throne
A wild romantic spirit he had shewn,
When in disguise, with Buckingham alone,
To Spain he journeys, with intent to see
The lady destined soon his bride to be.
Of dignified demeanour, not without reserve;
Such was King Charles, of whom we may observe
That arbitrary rule and unjust laws
Embroiled the country in the civil wars
Between the Parliament and King, whose will
Was that the former be considered nil.
Battle on battle followed till the end
At Naseby proved that longer to contend
Were vain; and Charles at last for refuge flies
To those he reckoned as his firm allies,
The Scottish army, who their sovereign sold
For some four hundred thousand pounds in gold.
Seldom has deed so treacherous and base
Been known a nation's annals to disgrace.
And prisoner of his Parliament is he
Who destined is its victim soon to be;
At Holmby seized, to Hampton Court then ta'en,
From thence escape contrived, but flight was vain;

---

* A.D. 1625.

He shelter seeks in Carisbrook's old walls,
And into his pursuers' power there falls,
Who after short debate the case decide,
Should by the Commons then with speed be tried;
And 'gainst the King the die was cast,
And death's stern sentence quickly passed.
A monarchy of nigh one thousand years
Kingless becomes, and no one there appears
The crown to claim, which had so fatal proved
* To Charles, for with it was his head removed.

Then with an altered aspect, strange yet true,
† Old England a republic next we view,
Governed alone by those who represent
The people, while the purpose and intent
Of prudent Cromwell, and of his intrigues,
Supported by some two-score more colleagues,
Whose power exerted ruthlessly destroyed
The House of Peers, and made it null and void;
Then 'twas that Cromwell formed a fresh resolve—
The faithful Commons likewise to dissolve,
Who for some thirteen years in union strong
Had formed the Parliament since known as Long.
As Lord Protector, then, his power was absolute,
Who only used the laws his plans to execute.
A general skilled, in whom his troops believed,
His arms abroad, at home success achieved.

---

* A.D. 1649.   † A.D. 1649.

In Ireland first he then rebellion stayed,
And 'gainst the Scots his skill likewise displayed,
Who under Leslie at Dunbar appear
Cromwell to face in the succeeding year.
And when again on Worcester's plain he meets
The second Charles, him then and there defeats,
Who, with his life in peril, forced to fly,
'Tis said concealed did in an oak tree lie;
That tree whereof the wooden walls were made
Which to the country proved a stout stockade.
And when the Dutch, also the Spanish fleet,
Were both with heavy losses bade retreat,
Some credit is certainly due to the ships
Which with judgment and care Old England equips;
And honour is likewise due to bold Blake,
Who more than a score of vessels did take,
While Oliver Cromwell's success against Spain,
Whereby he Jamaica and Dunkirk did gain,
Here duly we note at the end of his reign.
An exile from home 'tis that now they recall,
And into the place of his father install,
*A second King Charles, whose hist'ry begins
With a list of few virtues and manifold sins;
By nature a hypocrite, indolent, base,
A ruler who brought to his people disgrace;
Who given the manners and wit to attract,
Yet firmness of principle totally lacked.

* A.D. 1660.

To wit, that Dunkirk so lately acquired,
Again he returns as though it were hired;
And Louis of France delivers in gold
The price of the town which Charles to him sold.

'Twas then that the Dutch, who had suffered defeat,
Returned to the charge with a powerful fleet,
And entered the Medway as far as Sheerness,
In order that town for themselves to possess.
And burning the vessels that lay in their way,
They sailed up the Thames without further delay,
With the purpose old Tilbury's fort to attack;
But from hence by the English were soon driven back,
While Portsmouth and Plymouth resisted also,
Till a treaty of peace made friends of the foe,
And New Amsterdam just then changed its name
* For wedded to England, New York it became.

Then an *Archbishop murdered* proved the next cause
Of renewing in Scotland the Covenanters' wars,
Though Bothwell Bridge shewed a result so adverse
'Twere more than sufficient to make them disperse.

   But judgment with an iron hand
   Is now uplifted o'er the land;
   And all unseen from street to street
   The pale steed with his silent feet
      Performs his solemn round;

* A.D. 1669.

And no defence however strong
* Can stay him as he moves along,
   'Mongst the plague-stricken found
One hundred thousand there to claim
As victims, and those that remain
Full soon were called to view a sight
Which changed to-day the darksome night;
And suddenly afresh was spread
Wild terror with dismay and dread,
As from some hidden source outbreaks
The Fire-King, who the city rakes.
'Twas as if a depth volcanic,
Bursting, caused a fearsome panic,
And mad the fire is in its force,
Claiming the right to choose its course.
Awhile it levels with the ground
Whate'er may in that course be found.
Then houses, churches, vast St. Paul's,
Each one before the Fire-King falls,
And time alone can these restore
With greater fitness than before.

While the evil example of King and of Court,
Too soon yielded license for similar sport
'Mong those who when Puritans lately forswore
The follies forbidden now laid at their door.
But it boots not to dwell on deeds that offend
'Gainst the code of morality, or to extend

---

* A.D. 1665.

Our remarks on each latter event of a reign,
Which for plots and conspiracies famous became;
When the factions of Whig and of Tory uprose
To prove that the Court and the people were foes,
While political matters 'tis best to eschew,
For many they anger, and please but a few.

Now of the Stuart House remains
*The second monarch known as James;
By nature cruel, obstinate, severe,
In Council steady, faithful and sincere;
A Romanist, who therefore disagreed
With those on whom he would enforce his creed;
And they in dread lest he who rules the realm
No longer guides supreme the nation's helm,
But yields himself to the despotic sway
Of Papal power, which they will not obey.

†Then James of Monmouth dared the land invade,
And to the English crown his claim was laid,
But failing, suffered punishment condign,
As penalty for such a rash design;
Whose followers likewise shared his cruel fate
With little hesitation or debate,
For Jeffreys, who the law's stern arm then dealt,
Mercy nor clemency evinced or felt;
And seven reverend prelates, who demurred

---

* A.D. 1685.   † A.D. 1685.

To making known the Council's act and word,
Were sent to prison without being heard,
And though to freedom afterwards restored
I guess they were considerably floored ;
When James in turn for their assistance prayed,
And promises of some reform were made.
But Parliament at length resolved that he,
Foe to their faith, no longer King should be,
Who once already had from London fled,
And when brought back his life he held in dread.
By friends deserted, by his soldiers too,
No peace of mind the unhappy monarch knew.
What marvel, therefore, he should abdicate,
And then and there the English throne vacate,
Who seen departing one December morn,
Few looked on him with pity, more with scorn,
As silently adown the river glides
The royal barge, and James for shelter hides
In Gravesend's ancient town that night,
And then next day pursues his flight
Until at Rochester arrived,
* Escape from thence at length contrived,
Almost alone, devoid of state,
By secret stair and garden gate,
Thence to the boat, which waiting lay
Hard by, to speed him on his way,
In which they rowed him to Sheerness ;
A passage long and drear, I guess,

---

* A.D. 1688.

To take on a December night.
But soon the smack appeared in sight,
Whose tiny cabin then receives
A King, who throne and country leaves.
His bacon thus it was he saved,
While he the surging ocean braved,
And though old Neptune 'gainst him shews
His crested horses all in rows,
And caused the craft to pitch and reel,
Yet bacon fried a dainty meal
Proved for the King, who ate and drank
Right heartily, with cause to thank
His stars that he was safe and sound,
No longer treading English ground.
And then to England came the news
Landed was James at Ambleteuse,
Where France the fugitive receives,
An exile who his kingdom leaves.

   * Conjointly then the crown became
   Invested in a two-fold name;
   King William who as champion brave
   The cause of liberty to save,
   A Protestant, whose every deed
   Went to uphold th' established creed,
   And who, ere he held kingly sway,
   Landed an army at Torbay,

---

* A.D. 1689.

And Mary, daughter of the exiled James,
To share her husband's throne a title claims.
The interregnum passed, and both accept
The titled Majesty the late King left,
But which, desirous to regain,
Persistently he strove in vain,
Aided by Louis, King of France.
In Ireland landed he, to chance
Success among the Papists there,
And who in the rebellion share
Against the Protestants, their foes,
Who under Schomberg them oppose;
Then William and his followers join,
And fought the Battle of the Boyne,
In which King James they there defeat,
Who back to France then beats retreat;
And though the Catholics again
'Gainst William fought, 'twas all in vain;
The Toleration Act was passed,
And this their struggle was the last.

Now fain would we pass over the horrifying tale
Of deeds that desecrated a lone Argyleshire vale,
Where dwelt the clan Macdonald, whose character maligned,
To William represented as men no laws could bind;
And thus it was a paper of purport undefined
(Or what it meant he knew not) unwittingly he signed.
And armed with this same paper there marched into the glen
A neighbour chief commanding above one hundred men;

To meet a friendly welcome, as soldiers of the King,
From those but little dreaming destruction they would bring ;
Who were as guests respected, while full two weeks they passed,
Until the coward treachery was manifest at last.
When in the night's dark shadow they rose their hosts to slay,
While they all unsuspecting each wrapt in slumber lay.
Nor age, nor sex claimed mercy, not e'en the chief was spared.
Although so late the leader his home and fireside shared ;
In terror driven to perish abroad amid the snow
Some found in their last slumber a safety from the foe.
Meanwhile, the King knew nothing of this inhuman plot,*
For some three years kept secret, but ne'er to be forgot.
There is a trite old saying that murder sure will out,
Nor need we linger to inquire how there it came about ;
But he who Naboth-like aspired his neighbour's land to gain,†
To gaol was sent degraded, and well deserved the blame ;

---

* McArthur's History of Scotland, page 159. Whether William knew the whole state of the case or not when he signed the warrant is not certain, but he did not punish those who had dared to commit this wholesale murder in his name. And though four years after when a stir was made about it, he did grant a commission to the Privy Council to inquire into the matter, he did not bring to judgment the Master of Stair, who was very clearly pointed out as the guilty person. Page 187.

† Earl of Breadalbane. History of England, by the Rev. James White, page 660.

Which some would throw on William because he but complied
With what his Scottish councillors had chosen to decide.

Meanwhile his rule in England to us a progress shews,
Whereby her wealth and commerce yet more extensive grows;
A patriot and statesman, to whom the people owed
Their gratitude as tribute for benefits bestowed.
His principle was duty, their happiness his care,
The nation's great deliv'rer; few might with him compare.

Then to the House of Stuart we for a while return,
*And James the Second's daughter as Queen Anne we next discern.
In virtue of a faith reformed, the English throne she gains,
For lack of which the same was lost by her own father, James.
Coarse were the manners of the Queen, who needed cultivation
By that most truly potent power, the power of education;
But yet earned she a title to which all should here aspire,
Whether learning, wealth, or honour be their object or desire,
The sobriquet of "good" I mean,
Which so adorns the name of Queen.

'Twas then that mighty Marlborough the reputation made
For England as a nation with laurels ne'er to fade,

---

* A.D. 1702.

Whose victories in Holland, in Germany, and Spain,
Obtained the Peace of Utrecht, by treaty in this reign.
But lo! when the turmoil of warfare had ceased,
They found that the National Debt was increased,
And that brave men and true were not alone lost,
But that glory some twenty-one millions had cost;
And a treaty of commerce embodied likewise,
By which England from France might obtain her supplies,
By the Commons rejected, long afterwards proved
Perhaps the worst measure they ever had moved.
But now it behoves us our steps to retrace,
To note that 'twixt England and Scotland took place,
A union of their senatorial power
Which has e'en been upholden to this present hour;
And sixteen Peers, with Commons forty-five,
The Scottish jurisdiction kept alive
Amidst the stream of politics and strife,
Which in this reign unhappily were rife;
Till even Marlborough did they abuse,
And of an act of bribery accuse;
Although no bolder general e'er drew breath
Than he, who for his country oft faced death;
Who by a soldier's valour raised her fame,
And left himself an all undying name.

Now turn we to the last of good Queen Anne,
Whose reign not more than ten short years did span;
Yet men of varied genius brought to note,
Whose thoughts e'en still in books embodied float

Around about the world, to fertilise
The brains of men who would to genius rise,
*And Newton-like, to study e'en the skies,
And deep research known only to the wise;
While Locke and also Bacon then became
By genius honoured with immortal fame.
By loss of husband, loss of children tried,
Together Anne and House of Stuart died.

Established then, upon a basis sure,
The Protestant succession shall endure;
As now the House of Hanover, whose race
From the first James in retrospect we trace,
In England then assumed the royal sway,
Which it has held until the present day.
† And George, the Hanover Elector's son,
Who had no knowledge of the English tongue,
Simple in manners, and of person plain,
Commenced o'er Englishmen to rule and reign;
Frugal of habit, in deportment grave,
When called upon to fight a general brave.
Such was King George, who soon was forced to war
With James the Second's son, and rebel Mar;
Both he defeats, compelling a surrender,
And driving back the Chevalier Pretender.

---

* Sir Isaac Newton, mathematician and philosopher, born December 25th, 1642, died March 20th, 1726.

† A.D. 1714.

Then Knighthood's Order of the Bath became
Reward of valour, and for deeds of fame.
And on the sea success likewise attends
Old England's cause when she with Spain contends.
And these the facts connected with the name
Of George the First; but, spoken to his shame,
There is one other, namely, that he came
And lived, and reigned, and died alone,
While she who should have graced his throne
He prisoner made, and severed all the ties
Most sacred held, upon a base surmise.

Events political, increasing at this time,
Scarce can adapted be to suit our verse or rhyme;
Therefore this record now at once proceeds
* To George the Second, who the first succeeds.
In one chief point he, like his father, erred,
And Hanover to England much preferred.
But brave he was, who English soldiers led
At Dettingen, and conquered at their head,
Where by his side his second son,
Whose bold career had scarce begun,
He who as Duke of Cumberland was known,
His chivalry already here had shewn,
Which destined him hereafter to fulfil
The post of leader, which maintained he still
When the young Prince, Charles Edward, daring claims,

---

* A.D. 1727.

As grandson of the second Stuart James,
The land which his forefathers called their own,
Together with the right to England's throne.
'Twas then that Cumberland advanced to meet *
Prince Charlie, with intent him to defeat.
Long was the struggle, oftentimes renewed,
Between the rival armies that ensued;
Until at length, at Culloden, the fray
Proved fatal to the Prince, who lost the day.
Of Jacobites the last, with him the strife
Then ceased; but hunted for his life,
As some wild deer, who in his native glen
A monarch dwells, and shuns the haunts of men,
Until he bids "adieu" to Scotland's shore,
And sails for France, whence he returns no more.

Meanwhile the name of Cumberland is much belied
By those who had enlisted on the losing side,
And calumny recorded oft survives
Beyond the longest term of human lives.
But whether in it there be truth or not,
The foul aspersion still remains a blot
On whomsoever it be doomed to fall;
The same with prince or peasant as with all.

But next we mark how on the sea
England asserts her right to be

---

* "Life and Times of Prince Charles Stuart," by Alexander Charles Ewald, F.S.A.

Victorious, as in days of yore,
As ofttimes she had proved before,
While Anson's name at Finisterre *
Will long be well remembered there.
And Hawke also who at Bellisle,
Like him who later at the Nile,
A victory in triumph gains,
As hist'ry in due course explains.

Then forth there came a hero in Robert, first Lord Clive,
A heaven-born general truly, whose memory will survive
Long as the empire founded by his daring still is thine,
The home and pride of Englishmen, a star undimmed by time.
'Twas then the Earl of Chatham, the noble William Pitt,
Renowned alike for wisdom, no less than for his wit,
Lived as the honoured among men
No less than three-score years and ten,
And to obey whose proud behest
The gallant Wolfe sailed for the West,
In triumph there Quebec to take,
And a possession then to make
Of Canada for England's crown,
In gaining which he life laid down,

---

* Lord George Anson, who gained a victory over the French Admiral, Jouguière, near Cape Finisterre, in 1747.

Which life was for his country spent;
And inasmuch he died content.*
And ere some thirteen months were past
King George had likewise breathed his last.

† Then all the nation were concurred
To crown his grandson George the Third;
Who both his ancestors outvied,
And gloried with a manly pride
In that he spoke the British tongue,
And Britons e'er had dwelt among.
For some four hundred years and more
The crownèd heads of England bore
Title of King of France combined;
But such was wisely now resigned,
And George in courage and in zeal
Was mindful always of the weal
Of those o'er whom so long he reigned,
And of the kingdom which now gained
Their title new, by union planned
‡ With Britain Great and Ireland.

By nature generous and brave
Is he for whom we notice crave;

---

* General James Wolfe, when roused from fainting in the agonies of death by the sound of "They run," eagerly asked, "Who run?" and being told the French, he exclaimed, "Then I thank God and die contented." September 13th, 1759.

† A.D. 1761.   ‡ A.D. 1801.

A ruler prudent, affable, and kind
As any in these annals whom we find ;
And though in later years most sad his lot,
Let not the previous good be e'er forgot.

While in the reign of George the Third
A war with France again occurred ;
A war with victories replete,
Gained by the troops and by the fleet.
For though Napoleon's army passed
In triumph over Europe vast,
Britain, by skill, her power maintains,
And independent she remains,
Though to invade Napoleon planned,
And on the Kentish coast to land,
Until at length Trafalgar's fight
Left the French fleet in sorry plight,
Although the victors dearly paid
* For that which low their leader laid.

Of all that British troops befell,
This is no time or place to tell ;
For during some ten years or more
Abroad through Spain and France they bore
Their country's flag, till in the field
Of Waterloo, the Frenchmen yield,
And peace soon afterwards is sealed.

* A.D. 1805.

Within the memory of man
Are those events we have to scan.
In future, therefore, to be brief,
I'll touch on few, and those the chief;
Such as the fact that on the Clyde
Steam first to vessels was applied,
Which had already been decreed
Should hand-loom labour supersede;
And then to print in measured lines
The lengthy columns of the "Times."
* From Bath the coach known as the mail
Traversed the road, by hill and dale,
And tramcars 'gan to work by rail.
Then man bethought him he would try
If without wings he might not fly
(Presumption ever soareth high).
Now from beneath, and on the earth
Inventions ever new have birth,
But disappointment falls full soon
On those who trust to a balloon.

Time fails to tell of the great names
That grace one of the longest reigns
Which history's annals here record.
Some were made famous by the sword,
Others, by pencil or by pen,
Conveyed unto their fellow men

* A.D. 1784.

Results of study from their brains,
And each a recognition claims;
But 'tis with crownèd heads that we
Have most to do, and speedily.

In manners elegant and frank
As best became his royal rank,
* King George the Fourth, the eldest son
Of George the Third, might well have won
The honour and respect of those
Who afterwards became his foes;
Foes who by flattery mislead,
While youthful vanity they feed;
And his ill-treatment of the Queen his wife
Has cast a slur o'er his domestic life.
Now in this reign were speculations made,
Causing distress in commerce and in trade,
While country banks and London banks a few,
†Alike deceived, became by joint stocks new.
‡ 'Twas then the " Bobbies " organised their beats,
And gave protection to the London streets.
And said streets likewise they began to mend,
In that direction known as the West End.
Of London Bridge the first great stone was laid,
Which to this day stands firm and undecayed,
Thus few and salient are the points that need
Our wise remarks; then let us be agreed

---

* A.D. 1820.   † A.D. 1824.   ‡ A.D. 1831.

In charity, as doubtless it is best,
To bury faults, which Time has laid to rest.
And as the days when George the Fourth was King,
A living memory to some may bring,
Let us forbear invective or rebuke
And next pass on to him who once was Duke
Of Clarence, but who afterwards became
*The fourth King William, and the last whose name
As King of England figures here in space
Devoted to his great ancestral race.
And well-nigh eight long centuries have fled
Since England saw her Saxon monarchs dead,
And Norman sovereigns ruled and reigned instead,
Who since that time have numbered thirty-four;
They are not less, and may be some few more ;
If two or three short reigns we likewise count,
To seven-and-thirty swells the whole amount.

Now the remark must obvious be to all
That memories so recent to recall,
To say the least, would not be very wise,
And which to William as to George applies.
But of the chief events that happened then,
As they affect the rights of Englishmen,
That known as Parliamentary Reform
Without a doubt should e'er in mind be borne,

---

* A.D. 1831.

By which a Bill was added to the laws
That of a great excitement was the cause.

Then happened it, in two years more,
Namely, in eighteen thirty-four,
That to emancipate the slave
The nation twenty millions gave;
While there already had occurred
A change, which all the country stirred,
By means of locomotion new
That two great towns together drew;*
And through the kingdom's wide extent,
From John O'Groat's to coast of Kent,
The iron rails have since been laid,
Of which first trial then was made.

And 'mong the many names of note,
If time permitted we would quote,
Are men of science and of skill,
Memorials who have left, to fill
The world with an undying fame,
That e'er attaches to their name,
Who, benefactors of their kind,
Were gifted with inventive mind;
While others with the brush and pen
Sought to refine their fellow men.
And with an ear attuned to sound,
Musicians in this reign were found,

---

* Liverpool and Manchester Railway, opened September 15th, 1830.

Whose melodies still hold their place
For pathos and for finished grace.

Now, furthermore, we would but say
Of William, that when called to pay,
In eighteen thirty-seven, the debt
Of nature, let us not forget
That on that day commenced a reign
Which forms a bright link in the chain
To bind the present with the past;
And may it yet for years still last
Untarnished, as it ere has been,
United in our gracious Queen.

And now improvements multiplied
By sea and land on every side,
As in this coronation year,
Sailed for the Western hemisphere,
Two vessels first propelled by steam,
With great success, as it would seem,
For others followed in their track,
And made the distance there and back
With equal safety and with speed
Excelling those which took the lead.

Now henceforth to enumerate
Events so many and so great
As then occurred, I must decline,
And leave to other hands than mine.

But one, the Penny Postage Act,
An ever well remembered fact,
At this time came, its power to shew
In benefits to high and low;
And ready writers of the pen,
Now found in numbers among men,
Had not as much incentive, when
The interchange of mutual thought
On paper was more dearly bought.
Then in the year one eight five one,
A project to compare with none
The world's just admiration won,
And 'twas the Consort of the Queen
Its first promoter who had been—
Albert the Good, who well became
His honours and his honoured name.
He strove the nation to refine,
And here in union to combine
With others from afar, who brought
The works their industry had wrought,
And which, with many graceful arts
Allotted to their several parts,
A centre of attraction made
For visitors of every grade,
Who flocked in thousands to a scene
Compared with which none ere had been
So fair, so noble, or so grand,
In this or any other land.
And 'twas with most unfeigned regret,

Which none that witnessed could forget,
That, after some five months' display,
Which dated from the first of May,
The building closed one autumn day;
But not into oblivion falls
The spacious crystal roof and walls,
That, with the fittings and the floor,
On Sydenham Hall uprise once more,
And which we have described before,
When first our 'prentice hand we tried
To treat of subjects far and wide,
With what success you must decide.
Unbiassed may your judgment be
While having traced the pedigree
Of this colossal house of glass,
And which none other can surpass,
Our verse to those now we commend
Who have perused it to—THE END.

www.ingramcontent.com/pod-product-compliance
Lightning Source LLC
Chambersburg PA
CBHW020917230426
43666CB00008B/1479